HOLT McDOUGA

World History

PATTERNS OF INTERACTION

Guided Reading Workbooks
Answer Key

HOLT McDOUGAL
a division of Houghton Mifflin Harcourt

Peopling the Americas

SECTION 1

As You Read

Sample Answer: Australopithecines—upright walking, opposable thumb; *Homo erectus*—toolmaking, mastery of fire, language; Neanderthals—burial rituals, building of shelters; Cro-Magnons—advanced hunting and language skills.

Summary

1. The first humanlike beings, australopithecines, were found in East Africa. They lived about 3.6 million years ago.
2. The remains of *Homo habilis,* which means "man of skill," were found at a site that held tools of lava rock. *Homo habilis* lived about 2.5 million years ago. *Homo erectus* was the hominid that began to use tools for special purposes. *Homo erectus* may have also begun using fire, and they may have had the first spoken language.
3. Homo sapiens are modern humans. Early groups of humans lived in caves and built shelters. Their survival skills, ability to cooperate in hunting, and ability to speak set them apart from earlier hominids.

Graphic Organizer

Possible responses:
1. Australopithecines: opposable thumb; first to walk upright
2. *Homo habilis*: small brain; first toolmaker, butcher
3. *Homo erectus*: larger brain, more intelligent; first to use fire, spoken language, migrate
4. Neanderthals: heavy slanted brows, well-developed muscles, thick bones; developed religious beliefs, built temporary shelters
5. Cro-Magnons: identical to modern humans; planned difficult projects, communicated with language

Possible responses: Paleolithic Age: began 2.5 million B.C.; ended 8000 B.C.; made stone chopping tools Neolithic Age: began

8000 B.C.; ended 3000 B.C.; polished stone tools, made pottery, grew crops, raised animals

SECTION 2

As You Read

Sample Answer: Advances in Technology and Art: special spears, digging sticks, fish hooks, chisels, needles; necklaces, sculptures, cave and rock paintings. Beginnings of Agriculture: climate changed, longer growing seasons; slash-and-burn agriculture develops; animals domesticated. Villages Grow: Farming and herding allow settlements to flourish in river valleys in northeast Africa, China, Mexico and Central America, Peru, and Turkey.

Summary

1. Cro-Magnon tools and art showed the development of survival skills as well as the development of culture.
2. Farming developed. Animals were domesticated. The climate changed, and population increased.
3. Drought caused starvation. Floods and fires caused damage and death. Disease spread easily.

Graphic Organizer

Possible responses:
1. Used stone, bone, and wood to craft special tools to kill game, catch fish and pry plants loose
2. Necklaces, polished beads, carved sculptures of animals, cave paintings
3. Discovery that scattered seeds grew into crops, rising temperatures, rich supply of grain, food demands of small population boom
4. Developed in different places worldwide and spread from centers of agriculture to neighboring regions
5. Obsidian mirrors, jewelry, knives; colorful wall paintings; religious shrines
6. Natural disasters, disease, looting

SECTION 3

As You Read

Sample Answer: 1. advanced cities
2. specialized workers 3. complex institutions
4. record keeping 5. advanced technology

Summary

1. Villages grew. People were divided into social classes. Wealth and power were uneven.
2. The five features are advanced cities, specialized workers, complex institutions, record-keeping, and technology.
3. There were rulers and priests, traders, craft workers, and artists.

Graphic Organizer

Possible responses:

1. Economic changes: Irrigation systems, food surpluses, prosperous economy, new skills and crafts, expanded trade between villages
2. Social changes: Complex social relationships, development of social classes, more organized religion
3. Economic changes: Expansion of trade over a wider area, specialized workers, varied crafts, advanced technology
4. Social changes: Soaring populations, emergence of government to maintain order, system of writing to keep records, formal religious institutions

Early River Valley Civilizations

SECTION 1

As You Read

Sample Answer: Problems—Floods/climate, no natural barriers, limited resources. Solutions—Irrigation ditches, walled cities, trade with other groups.

Summary

1. The Sumerians dug irrigation ditches, built walls for defense, and traded food for the materials they needed.
2. Dynasties ruled the city-states.
3. Society was divided into social classes, including priests and kings, wealthy merchants, workers in the fields and workshops, and slaves.
4. Hammurabi's code made it clear that the government had some responsibility for the care of is people.

Graphic Organizer

Possible responses:

1. construct irrigation systems to carry river water to fields
2. build city walls with mud bricks
3. trade grain, cloth, and tools for products they lacked
4. give military leaders permanent control of standing armies and in turn city-states; set up dynasties
5. build ziggurats and offer sacrificed animals, food, and wine to the gods

Possible responses:

Religion: Polytheism, believed different gods controlled forces of nature
Literature: *The Epic of Gilgamesh*
Architecture: Ziggurats, arches, columns, ramps

SECTION 2

As You Read

Sample Answer: pyramids, mummification, hieroglyphic, written numbers, calendars, medicine; students may say that numbers and calendars were most important because of their lasting effects.

Summary

1. The Nile's delta defined Lower Egypt. The delta and the Nile's first area of cataracts marked the borders of Upper Egypt.
2. Pharaohs built pyramids because they believed they would rule the land after death.
3. Egyptian society consisted of the pharaoh and his family at the top. They were followed by people of wealth, priests, and members of the government and army. The middle class was next: merchants and crafts workers. At the bottom were peasants. Later, slaves formed a class below the peasants.

Graphic Organizer

Possible responses:

1. Menes united Upper and Lower Egypt.
2. Egyptian pharaohs were gods who ruled over government, religion, and the

military. Mesopotamian kings were representatives of gods, but they themselves were not considered gods.
3. Egyptians believed kings had eternal spirits and built pyramids as resting places from which their rulers could reign forever after death.
4. Both were polytheistic; Egyptians believed in an afterlife while Mesopotamians had a bleak view of death.
5. royal family; upper, middle, and lower classes; and slaves
6. developed a number system, form of geometry, columns in architecture, calendar, medical procedures, mummification
7. Both systems began with pictures to represent ideas.

SECTION 3
As You Read
Possible Answers: Cities: Central planning, advanced plumbing and sewage systems. Language: Written with symbols and phonetic sounds. Trade: Thriving trade by river, overland, and sea. Conclusion: The Indus Valley civilization had a high level of culture and organization.

Summary
1. People faced unpredictable floods, a changing river course and monsoons.
2. *Possible response:* They had planned cities; there were few differences between social classes; there was extensive trade with other areas.
3. The Indus River may have changed its course; the soil may have gradually become too poor to farm.

Graphic Organizer
Possible responses:
Geography: Hindu Kush, Karakoram, Himalaya ranges, and Indus-Ganges plain in north; desert in west; Deccan plateau in south; seasonal winds called monsoons
Settlements/Buildings: Planned cities with fortified citadel and uniform housing; brick buildings with plumbing and sewer systems

Religious beliefs: Worshiped major Indian god Shiva, mother goddess, fertility images, and cattle
Economic life: Farming, long-distance trade, production of nonessential goods; prosperous economy

SECTION 4
As You Read
Sample Answer: About 2,000 B.C.: First Chinese cities built. 1700 B.C.: Shang come to power (turning point because of cultural innovations). 1027 B.C.: Zhou come to power. 771 B.C.: Zhou Dynasty collapses.

Summary
1. China's mountains and deserts, as well as the ocean, kept it isolated.
2. Students may name any three: The Shang culture left the first written records, built buildings of wood, built walls around buildings, put the king and nobles inside city walls but left the peasants outside, and used wooden tools for farming.
3. Students may name any three: The Shang valued the group over the individual; respect for parents, the family, ancestors, and reading and writing.
4. The Zhou established the Mandate of Heaven and feudalism.

Graphic Organizer
Possible responses:
1. Huang He and Yangtze river systems, Plateau of Tibet, Gobi Desert, Mongolian Plateau, Himalaya Mountains
2. flooding of Huang He, geographic isolation
3. walled cities; elaborate palaces, tombs, timber-framed homes within city
4. warrior-nobles and peasants
5. central authority in Chinese society; elderly had special privileges; women treated as inferiors
6. worshipped spirits of family ancestors, supreme god, and lesser gods; consulted gods through oracle bones
7. many written characters, each representing an idea

8. manufactured weapons and religious items, bronzework
9. embroidered silk clothing

People and Ideas on the Move

SECTION 1
As You Read
Possible Answers: English, Spanish, Persian, Hindi, Sanskrit, Greek

Summary
1. Around 1700 B.C. they began to leave their homes and settle, in a series of migrations, in new regions.
2. They adopted some features and changed others. For example, they changed the laws to make them less harsh than Hammurabi's code had been.
3. This was an Aryan method of dividing people into classes with complex rules for how they could interact.

Graphic Organizer
Possible responses:
1. steppes
2. Anatolia
3. Babylon
4. chariots
5. iron
6. Aryans
7. castes
8. brahmins
9. untouchables or shudras
10. Magadha
11. and 12. Spanish, German, English, Persian, Sanskrit

SECTION 2
As You Read
Possible Answers: Hinduism: Caste system, many gods. Both: Reincarnation, enlightenment, cyclical history. Buddhism: Four Noble Truths, Middle Way.

Summary
1. Students may name any three: that each person has a soul, that Brahman brings together all individual souls, that souls are reincarnated, that people can eventually win escape from life on Earth, and that karma affects the next life.
2. Students may name any four: that the soul would be reborn, that the chain of new lives would continue until the soul reached understanding, that everything in life is suffering and sorrow, that the cause of suffering is desire for worldly pleasure, that the way to end suffering is to end desire, and that the Eightfold Path leads to nirvana.

Graphic Organizer
Possible responses:
1. Hinduism: Collection of religious beliefs that developed over time; no founder. Buddhism: Siddhartha Gautama.
2. Hinduism: Interconnectedness of all life; distinction between atman, soul of individuals, and Brahman, world soul; reincarnation of soul or spirit; good and bad karma; ultimate goal of moksha, state of perfect understanding. Buddhism: Four Noble Truths; an Eightfold Path to attain enlightenment; reincarnation, ultimate goal of nirvana, release from selfishness and pain.
3. Hinduism: Many gods including Brahma, the creator; Vishnu, the protector; Shiva, the destroyer; later, many forms of a great Mother Goddess. Buddhism: Enlightenment in place of many gods.
4. Hinduism: *Upanishads, Vedas.* Buddhism: Written teachings of Buddha, commentaries, rules about monastic life, how-to-meditate manuals, and Buddha legends.
5. Hinduism: Ideas of karma and reincarnation strengthened caste system. Hindu religion dominates daily activities. Buddhism: Rejected caste system; created religious communities of monks and nuns within society.
6. Hinduism: Freedom to choose among three paths for achieving moksha and the deity to worship. Buddhism: Daily declaration of "Three Jewels of Buddhism," pilgrimages to sites associated

with Buddha's life, performing of Buddhist worship rituals.

SECTION 3
As You Read
Possible Answers: Minoan: Traders (2000–1400 B.C.), bull leapers, potter. Phoenician: City-states, dye alphabet.

Summary
1. Three important features were the importance of trading; their art and architecture; and the high position of women.
2. The Phoenicians spread their culture through trade and through the establishment of colonies all along the Mediterranean coast. Phoenicians also spread their system of writing.
3. Trade networks were important because they connected the Mediterranean Sea with South and East Asia. People exchanged both goods and culture by means of these networks.

Graphic Organizer
Possible responses:
1. Minoans were a peaceful, not warlike, people, or they lived during a time of peace.
2. Minoans had some form of government and a culture that created and appreciated fine arts.
3. Women held a high rank in Minoan society; Minoans practiced organized religion.
4. The bull had special significance in Minoan history and culture.
5. The Phoenicians were skilled shipbuilders and sailors.
6. The Phoenicians were resourceful and skilled artisans.
7. Phoenician traders spread their alphabet system to the peoples with whom they traded.

SECTION 4
As You Read
Sample Answer: 1300 B.C. Moses: led the Israelites out of Egypt; 1200 B.C. Deborah:

unusual for a woman to be a leader; 1020–922 B.C. Saul: drove away the Philistines, David: united the tribes, Solomon: built a great temple.

Summary
1. Abraham was chosen by God to be the "father" of the Hebrews, ancestors of the Jewish people. He made the first covenant with God. He moved his family to Canaan.
2. The Ten Commandments are part of a code of laws that was, according to the Bible, delivered by God to Moses.
3. Israel was split into two kingdoms: Israel in the north and Judah in the south.
4. When the southern kingdom of the Jews was conquered by the Babylonians, the Jews were forced to move to Babylon. Eventually, they were allowed to return home.

Graphic Organizer
Possible responses:
1. the Torah
2. At first the Israelites held places of honor in the Egyptian kingdom, but later they were forced into slavery.
3. Moses led the Israelites out of slavery and received the Ten Commandments from God.
4. Saul drove the Philistines out of central Canaan; David united the tribes, made Jerusalem the capital, and began a dynasty.
5. to glorify God and house the Ark of the Covenant
6. High taxes and forced labor caused discontent resulting in the revolt of Israelites living in the northern part of the kingdom.
7. Chaldean king who twice attacked Jerusalem
8. Persian king Cyrus

First Age of Empires

SECTION 1
As You Read
1472 B.C.: Hatshepsut becomes pharaoh; 1285 B.C.: Battle of Kadesh; 1290–1224: B.C. Ramses II rules; 1200 B.C.: Kush regains

independence; 950–730 B.C.: Libyans rule; 671 B.C.: Assyrians rule Egypt.

Summary

1. Power struggles weakened Egypt, making the country vulnerable to the Hyksos and their chariots.
2. During the New Kingdom, pharaohs moved south and conquered Nubia.
3. The "Sea Peoples" and the Libyans
4. The Kushites accepted Egyptian culture and considered themselves its protectors.
5. The Kushite kings settled in Meroë. The city played an important role in trade and became a center for making iron weapons and tools.

Graphic Organizer

Possible responses:

1. around 1600 B.C.; helped drive Hyksos out of Egypt
2. around 1472 B.C.; encouraged trade
3. after death of Hatshepsut to around 1425 B.C.; built a mighty empire through victorious invasions into Palestine, Syria, and Nubia
4. about 1290 B.C.–1224 B.C.; made a treaty with Hittites that brought peace for rest of century; built great monuments including temple at Abu Simbel
5. 950 B.C.–730 B.C.; erected cities, established independent dynasties
6. 751 B.C.–671 B.C.; overthrew Libyan dynasty, united Nile Valley, established Twenty-fifth Dynasty

SECTION 2

As You Read

Sample Answer: Rise: 1. Need to defend against attacks; 2. Ironworking technology; 3. Advanced planning. Decline: 1. Hatred by conquered; 2. Overextension.

Summary

1. The Assyrians used different fighting methods, including bow and arrow, iron weapons, tunneling, and battering rams. They were also cruel and brutal.
2. The Assyrians built Nineveh, the largest city of its day. One king, Ashurbanipal,

gathered writing tablets from many lands. These would eventually provide historians with much information about ancient civilizations in Southwest Asia.

3. The Chaldeans were among the enemies of Assyria who helped capture Nineveh. They eventually took control of Mesopotamia.

Graphic Organizer

Possible responses:

Weapons and equipment: Iron-tipped spears and battering rams, daggers, and swords; armor and helmets, leather skirt with metal scales

Military tactics: Advance planning, which involved building bridges and weakening city walls; assaulting besieged city with arrows; ramming open gates and storming city

Method of governing: Organized conquered territories into a system of dependent provinces ruled by Assyrian officials or kings aligned with Assyria; used military power and cruelty to control empire.

Culture: Built magnificent cities and buildings, created fine carved sculptures, valued reading and writing

SECTION 3

As You Read

Sample answer: Cyrus only—Founded empire, let Jews return to Jerusalem. Darius only—Seized power, introduced coins of standard value. Both—Ruled fairly, expanded empire.

Summary

1. *Possible response:* Cyrus was an outstanding general, leader, and warrior. His military conquests formed a huge empire. He treated the conquered people respectfully and tolerantly. He lost his life in battle.
2. Darius created a government, divided the land into 20 provinces, put satraps in place, built the Royal Road, and created a common currency.
3. The Persians developed Zoroastrianism, which influenced later religions. They also brought political order to Southwest Asia

and provided a model for wise government.

Graphic Organizer
Possible responses:
King Cyrus: Founded Persian Empire
Allowed conquered people freedom
Allowed Jews to return to Jerusalem
Governed wisely and tolerantly
King Darius: Spent early years putting down revolts
Established organized, efficient government
Built system of roads
Introduced standardized money and promoted trade
Ruled with absolute power
Both: Military genius
Practiced tolerance
Honored customs and religions of "nationalities"

SECTION 4
As You Read
Sample answer: Philosophy—Confucius, Legalists, and Laozi offered solutions. Politics—Shi Huangdi enforced centralization. Cities—People moved there for protection.

Summary
1. He provided a model for ordered society and for good government.
2. To restore order in China
3. Shi Huangdi brought different parts of the empire together and doubled the size of China; took land from the wealthy; controlled ideas (and burned books); built a network of roads; set standards for writing, law, money, and weights and measures; and had the Great Wall built.

Graphic Organizer
Possible responses:
1. Confucius; social order should be based on basic relationships among people; education and a trained civil service essential for good government
2. Laozi; understanding nature is key to order and harmony; universal force called Dao guides all things

3. Hanfeizi, Li Si; efficient and powerful government is key to order; government should control ideas and use law and punishment to restore harmony

Classical Greece

SECTION 1
As You Read
Sample answer: Mycenaean—Strong rulers; Dorian—No writing.

Summary
1. Greece had few of its own natural resources.
2. The Mycenaeans borrowed from Minoan culture and adapted the Minoan form of writing and some forms of artistic decoration.
3. *Possible response:* People learned about the heroes of the Trojan War through Homer's great epic poem.

Graphic Organizer
Possible responses:
1. provided a transportation link for the various regions of Greece; connected Greece to other societies through trade
2. made unification difficult; created independent and isolated societies
3. resulted in a small population; created a need for colonies
4. developed an outdoor life for Greek males
5. adapted and spread Minoan culture, which later formed the core of Greek religious practice, politics, and literature
6. provided basis for legend and epic, may have contributed to collapse of Mycenaean civilization
7. led to a decline in economy, trade, and writing and to a period about which we know little, since written records were not kept

SECTION 2
As You Read
Sample Answer: Sparta: Conquers Messenia (725 B.C.), begins military state (about 650), Persian Wars (400s); Athens: Draco's Code (621 B.C.), enacts democratic reforms (500s),

Persian Wars (400s), dominates Delian League (470s).

Summary

1. Monarchy, aristocracy, or oligarchy.
2. Although all citizens could be part of government in Athens, only free adult males were citizens.
3. Sparta was a military state. It focused on war and being prepared for war.
4. After many battles, the Persians were defeated.

Graphic Organizer

Possible responses:

1. made them helots, peasants forced to stay on the land they worked and turn over half their crop
2. introduced timely reforms
3. strong, highly-disciplined military state
4. outlawed debt slavery, allowed all citizens to participate in Athenian assembly
5. allowed all citizens to introduce laws, created Council of Five Hundred chosen by lot to counsel assembly
6. discipline, training, heavy armor, and the phalanx formation
7. end of Persian threat and emergence of golden age of Athens

SECTION 3

As You Read

Sample Answer: strengthen democracy; strengthen empire; glorify Athens.

Summary

1. Pericles' goals were to make Athens more democratic, to make Athens stronger, and to make Athens beautiful.
2. To honor the Greek goddess Athena
3. Greek comedies made people laugh about important ideas.
4. Athens lost its empire.
5. Three important philosophers were Socrates, Plato, and Aristotle.

Graphic Organizer

Possible responses:

1. increased the number of paid public officials

2. built a strong navy, expanded overseas trade, bought expensive building materials, hired artisans to create works of classical art
3. love, hate, war, betrayal, hubris
4. discussed and accepted criticism of their ideas, behavior, customs, politics
5. Society would be divided into three groups—farmers and artisans, warriors, and the ruling class. The person in the ruling class with the greatest insight and intellect would be a philosopher-king.
6. scientific method

SECTION 4

As You Read

Sample Answer: I. A. builds army, B. conquers Greece. II. A. burns Persepolis, B. Darius found murdered.

Summary

1. Philip II of Macedonia conquered Greece.
2. Alexander conquered Persia and Egypt.
3. Alexander fell ill and died suddenly.

Graphic Organizer

Possible responses:

1. Goal(s): to carry out father's plan to conquer Persia
   Result(s): smashed Persian defenses at Granicus; alarmed Persian king Darius III, who raised huge army
2. Goal(s): to use surprise to overcome numerical disadvantage
   Result(s): gained control over Anatolia
3. Goal(s): to conquer entire Persian Empire
   Result(s): marched into Egypt, where he was welcomed as liberator and crowned pharaoh
4. Goal(s): to confront and destroy Persian king
   Result(s): ended Persia's power
5. Goal(s): to expand his empire eastward into India
   Result(s): won a battle against Indian army but weakened morale and exhausted troops forced a return to Babylon

SECTION 5

As You Read

Sample Answer: astronomy: planets rotate around Sun; geometry: Euclid's *Elements;* philosophy: virtue, moderation; art: realism.

Summary

1. Alexandria's was located on the Mediterranean Sea, had a good ship harbor, had lively trade, and a large population.
2. The pulley and the Archimedes screw
3. Hellenistic sculptures were more realistic and emotional.

Graphic Organizer

Possible responses:

1. Aristarchus concluded that the sun was larger than the earth and that the planets revolved around the sun; Eratosthenes used geometry to compute the earth's circumference; Ptolemy incorrectly concluded that the earth is the center of the solar system.
2. Euclid taught geometry and compiled a geometry text that is still the basis of courses in geometry; Archimedes calculated an approximate value of pi.
3. Archimedes invented the compound pulley to lift heavy objects and a device to raise water from the ground.
4. Zeno founded school of Stoicism whose ethical doctrine appealed to many different people. Epicurus founded Epicureanism, which taught that the greatest good and the highest pleasure came from virtuous conduct and absence of pain.

Ancient Rome and Early Christianity

SECTION 1

As You Read

Sample Answer: I. A. on river, B. Latins, Greeks, Etruscans. II. A. patricians and plebeians, B. written laws. III. A. thriving trade, B. Rove destroys Carthage.

Summary

1. Rome was on a river at the center of Italy and the midpoint of the Mediterranean Sea.
2. The three main parts were the consuls, the senate, and the assemblies.
3. Rome won control over Sicily, made Carthage a province, and made the Carthaginians slaves.

Graphic Organizer

Possible responses:

1. Rome developed because of its location on the Italian peninsula and its fertile soil.
2. The Romans adopted their alphabet and the use of the arch, and borrowed religious ideas from them.
3. patricians and plebeians
4. became basis for later Roman law and established the principle that free citizens had right to protection of the law
5. power struggle between Rome and Carthage for control of Sicily and western Mediterranean
6. attacked Carthage, forcing Hannibal to return home
7. gave Rome domination over western Mediterranean

SECTION 2

As You Read

Sample Answer: Increasing slavery; Gap between rich and poor; Christianity begins

Summary

1. Caesar governed as an absolute ruler. Some people mistrusted him, and some members of the senate murdered him. This led to a civil war and then the creation of the empire.
2. Most people were farmers. Other common occupations were traders and soldiers.
3. Slaves made up one-third of the population. Most slaves were people conquered by Rome. Slaves worked both in the city and on farms. Some slaves were gladiators.

Graphic Organizer

Possible responses:

1. agriculture, vast trading network, common coinage
2. government headed by emperor with a civil service to carry out day-to-day functions
3. discipline, strength, loyalty, practicality, usefulness
4. Slaves were numerous and important; and large differences in wealth and status separated social classes.
5. honored powerful gods and goddesses through rituals; emperor worship part of official religion
6. rich gave lavish banquets; masses attended free games, races, and gladiator contests

Possible responses:

1. Caesar emerged as a leader to bring order to Rome during a period of civil war. Later, when he defied the Senate, another civil war erupted. Yet another civil war followed his assassination.
2. Julius Caesar joined forces with Crassus and Pompey to form a triumvirate that controlled Rome for ten years. A Second Triumvirate ruled Rome after Julius Caesar was assassinated.
3. Caesar's success in conquering Gaul made him popular with the Romans.
4. Appointed dictator in 44 B.C., Caesar governed as an absolute ruler.
5. leaders of the Senate who assassinated Caesar

SECTION 3

As You Read

Sample Answer: Jesus of Nazareth, Jesus' death, Paul's mission, Constantine.

Summary

1. Roman leaders feared that Jesus would incite the people.
2. Drove many from their homeland; put to death many others
3. The pope was the bishop of Rome, later viewed as head of the Christian church. Below him were other bishops, with authority over all the individual churches in one area. Below them were priests, each in charge of a single church.

Graphic Organizer

Possible responses:

1. Christianity is based on the teachings of Jesus, who emphasized God's personal relationship to each human being. Jesus' simple message attracted great crowds, particularly among the poor, and many greeted him as the Messiah.
2. Jesus was born a Jew and his teachings contained many ideas from Jewish tradition, such as monotheism and the principles of the Ten Commandments.
3. Accused of challenging the authority of Rome, Jesus was crucified. After Jesus' death, his followers claimed to see him alive again, convincing them that he was the Messiah, or savior (*Christos* in Greek).
4. the first apostle; Jesus referred to him as the "rock" upon which the Christian Church would be built.
5. provided ideal conditions for travel and he exchange of ideas
6. In the Epistles and in his teachings, he stressed the universality of Christianity by declaring that the religion should welcome all converts.
7. ended persecution of the Christians in the Roman Empire and declared Christianity one of the religions approved by the emperor
8. made Christianity the empire's official religion

SECTION 4

As You Read

Sample Answer: Inflation: Coins had less value; Untrustworthy army: Mercenaries; Political instability: Bad economy, military turmoil.

Summary

1. Trade slowed, inflation occurred, and the food supply dropped.
2. Constantine was the Roman emperor who moved the capital to Byzantium and renamed the city Constantinople.

3. Attila led the Huns in terrorizing both eastern and western halves of the empire.

Graphic Organizer
Possible responses:
1. a. raids from hostile tribes and by pirates on the Mediterranean
   b. fewer lands to conquer and resources to gain
   c. To pay off debts, government raised taxes and coined more money with less silver, which led to inflation.
   d. recruitment of foreign mercenaries; fighting among military commanders for the throne
   e. declining economic, military, and social conditions
2. doubled size of Roman armies, fixed prices to control inflation, claimed descent from Roman gods, divided empire into eastern and western parts
3. extended reforms of Diocletian, restored concept of single ruler, moved capital from Rome to Byzantium
4. worsening internal conditions, invasions by Germanic tribes and Huns, separation of western empire from wealthier eastern part

SECTION 5
As You Read
Sample Answer: Fine Arts: sculpture, mosaics; Law: fair laws applied equally to all; Literature: Virgil, Ovid, Tacitus; Engineering: arch, dome, concrete.

Summary
1. Students may mention any three: sculpture, mosaics, paintings, the *Aeneid,* the histories of Tacitus.
2. Students may mention the ideas that all persons should be treated equally by law, a person is considered innocent until proven guilty, someone who accuses another of a crime has to prove it, and a person should be punished only for actions, not for thoughts or opinions.

Graphic Organizer
Possible responses:
1. Greek Contributions: provided model for fine art of sculpture. Roman Contributions: developed bas-relief, used mosaic tiles, created realistic portraits in stone, painted frescoes
2. Greek Contributions: Philosophers founded schools of philosophy, such as Stoicism, which encouraged virtue, duty, moderation, and endurance. Roman Contributions: applied teachings of Greek philosophers to administration of empire.
3. Greek Contributions: Provided forms and models for literary works, such as epics of Homer Roman Contributions: Wrote epics, as well as light, witty poetry and prose, especially history; used Roman themes and ideas in writing

Possible responses:
4. introduced and spread Latin, which remained the language of learning and of the Roman Catholic Church long after the Roman Empire fell
5. introduced arch, dome, and concrete; built Colosseum and other massive structures
6. built bridges, aqueducts, and extensive network of roads

India and China Establish Empires
SECTION 1
As You Read
Sample Answer: Mauryan—Unified and extended kingdom by force, required high taxes, promoted Buddhism and religious toleration; Gupta—Unified and extended kingdom by force, required high taxes, promoted culture.

Summary
1. Asoka ruled in a fair and just way, urging religious toleration. He built great roads so that people could travel easily.
2. The Tamils are southern Indian people. Their language is also called Tamil.
3. After the death of Chandra Gupta II, another wave of invaders moved into

India; the Gupta Empire broke into several smaller kingdoms.

Graphic Organizer
Possible responses:

1. The government levied high taxes on farmers and taxed income from trading, mining, and manufacturing.
2. He divided the empire into provinces, each headed by a royal prince, and further divided each province into local districts, whose carefully supervised officials assessed taxes and enforced laws.
3. He waged war to expand his power.
4. He tried to treat his subjects fairly and humanely and urged religious toleration. To improve communication throughout the empire, he built extensive road systems that were pleasant for travelers to use.
5. He consolidated an empire that included Magadha and the area just to the north of it, enabling him to use the strategic central region of the Ganges River as a power base.
6. He expanded the empire with forty years of conquest. He was also a supporter of the arts.
7. His defeat of the Shakas added their west coast territory to his empire, allowing the Guptas to expand trade between India and the Mediterranean world.
8. Using diplomatic and marriage alliances, he strengthened his empire.

SECTION 2
As You Read
Sample Answer: Religion: Hinduism, Buddhism; Arts: Literature, drama, music, dance; Science/Math: Number system, medicine; Trade: Overland and by sea to east and west.

Summary
1. The split in Buddhism made Buddhism a popular religion. This caused an increase in art: many shrines and temples were built, and artists were paid to decorate them with paintings and sculptures.

2. Scientists proved Earth was round and developed knowledge of disease and medicines. Mathematicians invented the idea of zero and decimal numbers.
3. India spread its culture, including its art, architecture, and religions, especially Buddhism.

Graphic Organizer
Possible responses:

1. The idea that many people could become Buddhas through good works changed Buddhism from a religion emphasizing individual discipline and self-denial to one that offered salvation to all and popular worship. Buddhists became divided into two sects over the new doctrines. The new trends also inspired Indian art.
2. A trend toward monotheism developed. Although Hinduism embraced hundreds of gods, many Hindus began to devote themselves to Vishnu or Shiva. As Hinduism became more personal, it also became more appealing to the masses.
3. Writing academies were formed in the city of Madurai, and more than 2,000 Tamil poems from this period still exist. Dance and drama became popular.
4. Indians began to use a calendar based on cycles of the sun, a seven-day week, and a day divided into hours. Scientists proved that the earth was round by observing a lunar eclipse. Numerals (including zero) and the decimal system were invented and mathematicians calculated both the value of pi and the length of a solar year to several decimal places.
5. Indian traders worked as middlemen, buying Chinese goods and selling them to traders traveling along the Silk Road to Rome. The Indians also built trading stations along the roads. The sea routes allowed Indian traders to develop or expand trade with merchants in Africa, Arabia, and China. Indians would sail to Southeast Asia to collect spices, bring the spices back to India, and sell them to Roman merchants.

6. Increased trade led to the rise of banking in India. Indian merchants who moved abroad helped spread Indian culture throughout Asia.

SECTION 3
As You Read
Sample Answer: I. A. centralized government, B. peace and stability, C. expanded empire. II. A. clear levels in society, B. civil service. III. A. advances in technology, B. agriculture primary, C. silk trade established.

Summary
1. Liu Bang started a centralized government, lowered taxes, and decreased punishments for crimes.
2. The population had grown greatly.
3. The peasants rebelled because they were forced to pay high taxes and lived poor lives.

Graphic Organizer
Possible responses:
1. established centralized government of top-down rule in which Liu Bang had authority over all; lowered taxes, eased harsh punishments, brought stability and peace to China
2. controlled the throne by naming one infant after another as emperor and acted as regent for each
3. conquered lands and made allies of the enemies of his enemies; set up a civil service system of training and examinations for those who wanted government careers
4. minted new money to relieve the treasury's shortage, established public granaries to feed the poor, and tried to redistribute land from the rich to the poor

Possible responses:
5. increased availability of books, helped spread education, promoted expansion of government bureaucracy by producing records that could be more easily read and stored

6. helped to create a worldwide demand for silk and expanded Chinese commerce all the way to Rome
7. Government recognizes need to unify the empire and promotes various methods of assimilation (e.g., intermarriage, schools to teach conquered peoples, appointing local people to government posts).
8. Political instability increases. Economic weaknesses and imbalance topple the empire.

African Civilizations

SECTION 1
As You Read
Sample Answer: I. A. Challenging Environments, B. Welcoming Lands. II. A. Nomadic Lifestyle, B. Transition to a Settled Lifestyle. III. A. Local Religions, B. Keeping a History. IV. A. The Nok Culture, B. Djenné-Djeno.

Summary
1. Students may name any three: a huge coastline but few harbors, harsh desert covering one-third of the continent, wet rain forests; high, cool mountains, high plateau, unnavigable rivers, savannas.
2. They farmed an area near the Sahara, the Nile Valley, West Africa, and the grasslands.
3. The common features were that the family was the most important social unit; a belief in one god as creator and animism; and a reliance on the oral tradition.
4. Djenné-Djeno is the oldest known African city south of the Sahara. It dates from 250 B.C.

Graphic Organizer
Possible responses:
1. made navigation impossible to and from the coast; isolated groups who lived inland by limiting their contact and trade with other groups living along the rivers or on the coast
2. hampered movement of peoples; mostly too hostile for people to inhabit

3. fertile land and mild climate supported large population of farmers and herders along the northern coast

4. prevented use of draft animals in farming near rain forests; also prevented invaders from colonizing fly-infested territories

5. supported abundant farming and herding that led to permanent settlements on the grassy plains, healthier lives, and increased birthrates

Possible responses:

6. remained hunter-gatherers; learned to identify and use resources of natural environment

7. farmed; must have mined nearby iron because they learned smelting to make iron tools for farming and iron weapons for hunting

8. fished in Niger River, raised rice and herded cattle on fertile floodplains, became prosperous through trade on Niger and overland camel routes

SECTION 2
As You Read
Sample Answer: Effects: ironworking spread, Bantu language/culture spread, population spread.

Summary
1. Three reasons are environmental change, economic pressure, political and religious persecution.
2. *Possible response:* Reasons included farming methods that depleted the soil, increased population, and clashes with other peoples.

Graphic Organizer
Possible responses:
1. a. They farmed only along riverbanks.
   b. These were the only places that had enough sun.
2. a. They adapted techniques of herding goats and sheep to raising cattle.
   b. The savannas could support cattle.
3. When their farming methods or the new crops they learned to cultivate had

exhausted the land, the people had to pick up and migrate to another place.
4. a. The area to the north was already densely populated and the desert was expanding southward.
   b. In territorial wars, the newcomers, with their superior weapons, drove the non-Bantu-speakers into small areas.
5. a. They exchanged ideas and intermarried with the original people. b. The intermingling created new cultures with unique customs and traditions.
6. As a result of Bantu migrations, today there are at least 60 million people who speak one of the Bantu languages.

SECTION 3
As You Read
Sample Answer: Christianity; trade networks; architecture; terracing.

Summary
1. Aksum's trade routes helped link Rome to India. It was a hub of world trade.
2. Advances and achievements included building out of stone, creating pillars, having a written language, and using new methods of farming.
3. After Islam conquerors destroyed Adulis, the capital was moved to a hard-to-reach area over the mountains in what is now northern Ethiopia.

Graphic Organizer
Possible responses:
1. Aksum's location and expansion made it an important trading center.
2. Merchants exchanged raw materials, goods, and ideas. Among the latter was the idea of Christianity.
3. Their land was hilly.
4. The conquest cut Aksum off from its major ports and the kingdom declined as an international trading power. The spread of Islam isolated Aksum from other Christian settlements.
5. To escape the Muslims, Aksum's leaders moved their capital to an isolated area over the mountains.

The Americas: A Separate World

SECTION 1

As You Read

Sample answer: Cause 1: Beringia land bridge forms. Effect 1: Siberian hunters enter North America. Cause 2: Experiments with farming begin. Effect 2: Crops provide reliable food supply.

Summary

1. They came from Asia across the land bridge that existed during the last Ice Age.
2. They hunted mammoth, deer, rabbits and other small mammals
3. Maize grew so well that a family of three could, in four months, grow enough corn to feed it for two years.

Graphic Organizer

Possible responses:

1. toward the end of the last Ice Age, by foot over a land bridge from Asia or in small boats
2. hunted smaller prey, fished, and gathered edible plants and fruits
3. People began planting and harvesting preferred edible plants from seeds.
4. maize, squashes, beans, avocados, chilies
5. With a reliable food supply, people settled in permanent villages.
6. Nonagricultural activities and skills developed, creating social classes.

SECTION 2

As You Read

Sample answer: Olmec: May have rafted monuments along waterways, worshiped jaguar spirit, traded with faraway regions. Both: Built huge monuments, decline mysterious. Zapotec: Built urban center.

Summary

1. Archaeologists have found mounds, courtyards, pyramids, columns, altars, and stone heads and other monuments left by the Olmec.
2. Archaeologists have found evidence of stone platforms, temples, writing, a

calendar, a large city, pyramids, palaces, and an observatory.

3. The Zapotec way of writing and calendar were taken by other groups, and the city of Monte Alban influenced other cities in the region.

Graphic Organizer

Possible responses:

1. located along Gulf Coast of Mexico, covered with swamps and rain forest and fertile river flood plains; hot and humid climate; abundant resources of salt and tar, clay, wood, rubber
2. combined pyramids, plazas, and giant sculptures; built thriving urban communities at sites such as San Lorenzo and La Venta
3. directed a large and prosperous trading network throughout Mesoamerica
4. jaguar motif and other art styles; pattern of urban design; concepts of ceremonial centers, ritual ball games, and a ruling class
5. located in mountainous region in southern Mexico; fertile soil and mild climate in valleys
6. planned cities with stone pyramids, temples, and palaces built around a giant plaza
7. hieroglyphic writing system
8. concept of urban planning; calendar system based on movements of the sun

SECTION 3

As You Read

Sample answer: Chavín: 900–200 B.C.; Andes Mountains; carvings, pottery, textiles. Nazca: 200 B.C.–A.D. 600; Peruvian coast; irrigation, textiles, pottery, Nazca lines. Moche: A.D. 100–700; northern coast of Peru; irrigation, jewelery, pottery.

Summary

1. Scientists think that Chavin culture helped shape other cultures to the north and south of its site. They also think the main site was not the center of a political empire but the chief site of a spiritual or religious movement.

2. *Possible responses:* The Moche people built ditches to bring water to their fields; they raised several crops; they fished and hunted. They had great wealth and made beautiful pottery.

Graphic Organizer
Possible responses:
1. Chavín: highland region of Peru; 900 B.C. to 200 B.C.; religious images reflected in stone carving, pottery, and textiles; religious centers featuring pyramids, plazas, and giant earthen mounds
2. Nazca: dry southern coast of Peru; 200 B.C. to A.D. 600; extensive irrigation systems, textiles and pottery with images of animals and mythological beings, Nazca Lines
3. Moche: northern coast of Peru, watered by rivers flowing from Andes; A.D. 100 to A.D. 700; irrigation systems, ceramic pottery, beautifully crafted gold and silver jewelry, musical instruments, woven clothing, tombs

The Muslim World

SECTION 1
As You Read
Sample answer: Events: Divine revelations, Hijrah, Mecca captured. Beliefs: Allah, Five Pillars, tolerance of Jews and Christians. Sources: Allah, Qur'an, Sunna. Beginning: Gabriel's visitation.

Summary
1. By the early 600s, trade became important because people had begun to live in towns and cities and making a living was difficult in the desert.
2. The Hijrah was the movement of Muhammad and his followers from Mecca to Yathrib in 622. This marked a turning point for Muhammad, after which he and his followers gradually gained power.
3. The five duties are to state a belief in Allah, and Muhammad, his prophet; praying to Allah five times a day; giving alms to the poor; fasting during Ramadan;

performing a hajj to Mecca at least once in a lifetime.

Graphic Organizer
Possible responses:
1. He believed that God, also known as Allah, spoke to him through the angel Gabriel. As a result of this experience, Muhammad came to believe that he was the last of the prophets and had to teach others that Allah was the one and only God and that all other gods must be abandoned.
2. Meccans feared that traditional Arab gods would be neglected and that Mecca would no longer be a center for pilgrims.
3. Muhammad attracted devoted followers and became a popular religious leader; a political leader who began unifiying the Arabian Peninsula under Islam; and a military leader in the hostilities between Medina and Mecca.
4. Muhammad used Mecca as a base from which to gain loyal converts to Islam.
5. There is only one God, Allah; each person is responsible for his or her own actions.
6. Muslims do not separate their personal life from their religious life. Carrying out the Five Pillars of Islam and other customs ensures that Muslims live their religion while serving in their communities.
7. Because the Qur'an was written in Arabic, that language spread widely as Muslims expanded into many lands.
8. Shari'a law required Muslims to extend religious tolerance to Christians and Jews.

SECTION 2
As You Read
Sample answer: Rightly guided caliphs: 632–661; spread of Islam east and west, tolerance of Jews and Christians. Umayyads: 661–750; split between Sunni and Shi'a, development of Sufi movement. Abbasids: 750–1258; shift of capital to Baghdad, growth of a trade network.

Summary
1. Abu–Bakr spread Islam through battle and conquest.

2. The Shi'a and Sunni groups developed in reaction to beliefs about the caliph. The Shi'a believed caliphs had to be relatives of Muhammad. The Sunni accepted other caliphs.

3. The Abbasids overthrew the Umayyads and built the city of Baghdad as their capital. The Abbasid caliphate was in power for just over 500 years.

Graphic Organizer

Possible responses:

1. the Qu'ran and Muhammad's actions

2. They mobilized highly disciplined armies that conquered Arabia, parts of the Byzantine Empire, and parts of the Sassanid Empire.

3. Muslims were willing to fight to extend and defend Islam; armies were well disciplined and expertly commanded; Byzantine and Sassanid empires were weak; people who had suffered from religious persecution welcomed the more tolerant invaders.

4. the assassination of Ali and the rise to power of the Umayyads

5. moved the capital, abandoned the simple life of previous caliphs, and surrounded themselves with wealth and ceremony

6. vigorous religious and political opposition

7. They were the most powerful of the rebel groups that opposed the Umayyads; as such, they took control of the empire.

8. moved the capital to a newly created city, Baghdad; developed strong bureaucracy to conduct the affairs of the huge empire; created a system of taxation; established strong trade network

9. failed to keep complete political control over their immense empire

SECTION 3

As You Read

Sample answer: Science and Math: translated Greek scientific texts, conducted experiments in laboratory settings, began the study of algebra, advanced the field of astronomy. City life: Cities were centers of learning that produced skilled bureaucrats and officials

needed to run a vast empire. Society: four social classes: upper class (born as Muslims), second class (Muslim converts), third class ("protected people" such as Christians, Jews, and Zoroastrians), fourth class (slaves). Arts and Literature: calligraphy and the decorative arts, mosque architecture, poetry, popular literature, such as *The Thousand and One Nights.*

Summary

1. The four groups were: 1. Muslims by birth; 2. those who converted to Islam; 3. Jews, Christians, and Zoroastrians; 4. slaves.

2. Muslim scholars collected ancient Greek, Indian, and Persian works of science and philosophy and translated them into Arabic. During the Middle Ages, much of this knowledge was lost in Europe, but it was preserved by Muslim scholars and later returned to Europe.

3. Four achievements include an encyclopedia of medicine, the use of logic to test ideas, discoveries about how people see, and the development of algebra.

4. He tried to blend the ideas of the ancient Greek philosophers with those of Islam.

Graphic Organizer

Possible responses:

1. Four social classes: birth Muslims, converts, those of other religions (called "protected people"), and slaves. Muslim women had more rights than European women of the same time. Their responsibilities varied depending on their husband's income, but all women were responsible for raising children. Construction of Baghdad symbolized the strength of the Abbasids.

2. Muslim scholars introduced to modern math and science important concepts: reliance on scientific observation and experimentation and the ability to find mathematical solutions to old problems. They wrote important medical reference books; developed algebra and used mathematical advances in astronomy; used an astrolabe; charted stars, comets, and

planets; and produced a book about optics that laid the basis for the development of the telescope and microscope lenses.

3. Scholars translated works of Greek philosophers into Arabic. Ibn Rushd tried to blend Greek views with those of Islam.

4. The Qur'an is the standard for literature; poetry was important; stories included *The Thousand and One Nights*.

Byzantines, Russians, and Turks Interact

SECTION 1
As You Read
Sample answer: Retook most of the Western Empire from Germanic groups; oversaw the revamping of Roman law—the Justinian Code; launched massive building campaign to create a dazzling imperial capital; preserved Greco-Roman culture.

Summary
1. Justinian was the Byzantine emperor who restored almost all of the old Roman empire's territory.

2. Justinian built walls for protection; a huge palace; and many public buildings. He also rebuilt Hagia Sofia to make it the most beautiful church in the Christian world.

3. The biggest threats were repeated and devastating illness, and attacks from German tribes, Sassanid Persians, and Muslim armies.

4. Students may name any two: The Eastern Church is led by a patriarch; Rome by a pope; the Eastern Church uses icons; the Roman Church does not; the languages of the two groups differ; the cultures of the two groups differ.

Graphic Organizer
Possible responses:
1. conquered new lands so that he ruled a territory almost as great as Rome's had been; his legal experts completed creation of a body of civil law, called the Justinian

Code; rebuilt Constantinople, built Hagia Sophia

2. It killed so many people that it left the empire severely weakened and exposed to its enemies.

3. At first, they used bribes, diplomacy, and political marriage. Then they reorganized the empire along military lines.

4. There were irreconcilable differences between the two traditions in language, church authority, divorce, and priests' right to marry. Finally, the pope and patriarch excommunicated each other in a dispute over religious doctrine.

5. Christianity was permanently divided between the Roman Catholic Church in the west and the Orthodox Church in the east.

6. its walls, fleet, and strategic location

SECTION 2
As You Read
Sample answer: Nobles: Collected tribute; put down revolts. Church: Accepted Mongols; mediated between Mongols and Russians. People: Paid high taxes; Princes: Collected taxes; controlled small states.

Summary
1. Olga and Vladimir spurred the conversion of the Slavs to Christianity.

2. Yaroslav's sons fought one another for power; trade declined.

3. It isolated the Russians from western Europe, causing Russian society to develop in its own way; it united many different areas of Russia; it led to the rise of Moscow.

Graphic Organizer
Possible responses:
1. trade by easy river and sea route; religion after 989

2. Vladimir expanded the state west into Poland and north almost to the Baltic Sea. Yaroslav married off his daughters and sisters to the kings and princes of Western Europe to forge important trading alliances. He created a legal code tailored

to Kiev's commercial culture and built a library and churches.

3. Yaroslav divided his realm among his sons. They tore the state apart fighting for territory. This system of dividing continued through several generations. The Crusades disrupted trade, and the Mongols attacked and demolished Kiev.

4. tolerated all religions; allowed Russians to follow usual customs; demanded obedience and large amounts of tribute from all principalities

5. isolated Russia more from Western Europe; encouraged the rise of Moscow as a center of power; encouraged the guidance and control of the Byzantine Church

6. Czar Ivan III refused to pay tribute to the Mongols; as a result, Russian and Mongol armies had a bloodless standoff.

SECTION 3
As You Read
Sample answer: Abbasids: Took slaves; Persians: Took control from caliph; Seljuks: Adopted Persian culture; Mongols: Killed opposition, destroyed property.

Summary
1. The Seljuks relied on the government experience of Persians. They placed their capital in Persian lands. They also adopted Persian culture, including the proper way to follow Islam and the Persian language.
2. The empire was weakened by weak rulers and by the Crusades. It was ended by Mongol invasion.

Graphic Organizer
Possible responses:
1. They put an end to the caliph's political power.
2. They converted to Islam but continued to make war on other Muslims.
3. The Turks crushed the Byzantines at the Battle of Manzikert in 1071. Within the year, they occupied all of Anatolia and were close to Constantinople.
4. This political move helped the Turks win the support of their Persian subjects.

5. The Arabic language almost disappeared from Persia, except among religious scholars.
6. No capable shah replaced him, and the Seljuk Empire quickly disintegrated into a collection of petty kingdoms.
7. Led by Saladin, the Muslims recovered Jerusalem from the Christians and signed a truce with King Richard I of England.
8. The threat to the Turks from the west eventually subsided.

Empires in East Asia

SECTION 1
As You Read
Sample answer: Tang: Expanded China; Song: Lost territory and paid tribute; Both: Founded eras of stability and prosperity.

Summary
1. Tang rulers made the government stronger and brought back the practice of hiring Confucian scholars to run the empire.
2. The Song Dynasty took the place of the Tang.
3. Possible responses: movable type, gunpowder, advances in farming, and development of an improved variety of fast-growing rice.
4. The old noble families lost power, and the gentry gained power. Women lost power.

Graphic Organizer
Possible responses:
1. expanded network of roads and canals begun by Sui Dynasty
2. strengthened central government, revived and expanded civil service
3. encouraged extensive overland foreign trade and expanded sea trade; colonies; resulted in the introduction of new religions, including Buddhism, Islam, and some Eastern sects of Christianity
4. improved the cultivation of rice
5. developed movable type, gunpowder, magnetic compass
6. nurtured work of artists, produced great poetry and painting
7. power began to fade

8. created this elite upper class whose status was based on education and position in civil service, not land ownership

9. status declined, especially among upper classes in cities; introduced custom of foot-binding

SECTION 2
As You Read
Sample answer: Genghis Khan unites Mongols by 1206; Mongols control Central Asia by 1225; Genghis's successors conquer territory from China to Poland in 50 years after his death.

Summary
1. Students may name any three: herding animals, traveling from place to place, living on horseback, traveling in groups, living in clans, and sporadic attacks on settled peoples.
2. Well-organized army; Genghis Khan's own ability to outwit his enemies; and their use of cruelty as a weapon.
3. *Possible responses:* a period of peace; increased trade; an exchange of ideas with Europe.

Graphic Organizer
Possible responses:
1. Because of scarcities and the hardships of their lifestyle, steppe Nomads raided towns and villages to acquire pasture land for their herds and resources for survival.
2. fought and defeated his rivals, one by one
3. He was a brilliant organizer, gifted military strategist, and a cruel terrorist.
4. Great Khan (China), Khanate of Chagatai (Central Asia), Ilkhanate (Persia), and the Khanate of the Golden Horde (Russia)
5. At first, they ruled ruthlessly, destroying the land and irrigation systems and wiping out populations; later they adopted aspects of the cultures they ruled and imposed stability and law and order across much of Eurasia.
6. contributed to its splitting up
7. From the mid-1200s to the mid-1300s, the Mongols established stability and law throughout much of Eurasia.

8. made travel and trade safer and fostered the exchange of goods and ideas across Asia and Europe

SECTION 3
As You Read
Sample answer: Tolerated Chinese culture; Promoted trade, which made China stronger; Failed to conquer Japan; May have employed Marco Polo.

Summary
1. The Yuan Dynasty united China for the first time in three centuries. It also opened China to trade with the West.
2. Kublai Khan rebuilt the Great Canal and promoted foreign trade.
3. *Possible responses:* failed attacks in Southeast Asia were costly; high taxes caused hardship; fighting among leaders weakened Mongol rule.

Graphic Organizer
Possible responses:
1. grandson of Genghis Khan, known as the Great Khan, united China for the first time in 300 years Venetian trader who traveled to China, visited Kublai Khan's court, and then served Kublai Khan for 17 years
2. 1279, 1260–1294
3. Shangdu and modern-day Beijing from Mongolia to China
4. kept their Mongol identity; tolerated Chinese culture, retained Chinese officials in local governments made caravan routes across Asia safe, established mail routes to link China with India and Persia, greatly improved trade, and invited foreign merchants to visit China
5. They believed that foreigners were more trustworthy than Chinese since they had no local loyalties. Storms destroyed two invading fleets. It united China, expanded foreign contacts, and made few changes to Chinese culture and system of government.
6. civil discontent because of famine, floods, and disease; economic problems and official corruption; power struggles among

Yuan family members; rebellions of
Chinese

SECTION 4
As You Read
Sample answer: Yamamoto leading clan by
400s; First of many missions to learn from
China in 607; Court accepts Buddhism in the
mid-700s; Court moves to Heian in late 700s
and Heian period (794–1185) begins; Central
power of the Fujiwara begins to slip in the
mid-11th century; Kamakura shogunate of the
1200s repulses naval invasions of Kublai Khan
in 1274 and 1281.

Summary
1. The Yamato were a powerful clan. Its
   leaders began to call themselves emperors.
2. *Possible responses:* Buddhism, the
   Chinese system of writing
3. Samurai were trained soldiers who
   protected lords from attacks by other
   lords.

Graphic Organizer
Possible responses:
1. in early history, isolated Japan from
   invasion but allowed cultural borrowing
   from China; limited fertile land and
   natural resources
2. established concept of dual structure of
   government—an emperor who reigned and
   a power behind the throne who actually
   ruled—which became an enduring
   characteristic of Japanese government
3. introduced Chinese ideas and customs,
   including Buddhism and Chinese system
   of writing
4. influenced religious life (with the
   introduction of Buddhism); artistic styles;
   simple arts of daily living such as cooking,
   gardening, drinking tea, and hairdressing;
   and early government
5. refined court society
6. strengthened localized rule of lords over
   central government
7. transferred real center of power to military
   headquarters where shoguns ruled as
   dictators through puppet emperors

SECTION 5
As You Read
Sample answer: Khmer—Built Angkor Wat;
Dai Viet—Women had more freedom then
Chinese women; Korea—Occupied by
Mongols; Sailendra—Built temple at
Borobudur; Srivijaya—taxed trade.

Summary
1. The Srivijaya Empire and Dai Viet
2. The Koryu was the dynasty that ruled
   Korea from 935 to 1392 and which
   produced many great artistic
   achievements.

Graphic Organizer
Possible responses:
1. modern-day Cambodia improved rice
   cultivation, built Angkor Wat and other
   city-and-temple complexes, became main
   power on Southeast Asian mainland
2. Java—constructed massive Buddhist
   temple at Borobodur and other
   architectural monuments
3. Sumatra, Borneo, and Java as well as the
   waters of the Strait of Malacca gained
   wealth by taxing trade through Strait of
   Malacca; set up center of Buddhist
   learning in Palembang, their capital on
   Sumatra
4. Vietnam—located capital at Hanoi,
   established strong central government,
   encouraged agriculture and trade,
   improved road and river transportation
5. Korea—established Confucian civil
   service examination system; produced
   celadon pottery and large wooden blocks
   for printing all of the Buddhist scriptures

Possible responses:
Indian: Hindu and Buddhist practices, Indian
political ideas, languages, art forms
Chinese: Buddhism, Confucianism, concept of
centralized government and civil service,
writing system, porcelain pottery

European Middle Ages

SECTION 1
As You Read
Sample answer: 400s: Roman Empire invaded; 511: Clovis unites Franks in Christian kingdom; 590: Gregory the Great becomes pope; 732: Charles Martel defeats Muslim raiders; 751: Carolingian Dynasty begins; 800: Pope crowns Charlemagne emperor; 800s: French, Spanish, and other languages evolved from Latin.

Summary
1. *Possible response:* The end of trade, the decreasing importance of cities, movement to rural areas, decreasing level of education, development of various dialects.
2. A new kind of government arose based on family ties and loyalty to a local leader.
3. Monasteries acted as religious communities and centers of learning.
4. Charles Martel was the Frankish mayor of the palace who ended the Muslim threat to Europe. His son, Charles Pepin, began the reign of Frankish rulers called the Carolingian Dynasty.
5. The crowning of Charlemagne marked the joining of the pope's power, the Franks' power, and the heritage of the Roman Empire.

Graphic Organizer
Possible responses:
1. After Clovis's conversion, the Church supported his military campaigns against other Germanic peoples.
2. He broadened the Church's power to include secular affairs and spread the idea of a churchly kingdom.
3. The victory halted a Muslim invasion, prevented the Frankish kingdom from becoming part of the Muslim Empire, and made him a hero.
4. He successfully fought the Lombards and was anointed by the pope, establishing an informal alliance between the pope and Frankish kings.

5. The event signaled the joining of Germanic power, the Church, and the heritage of the Roman Empire.
6. He sent out agents to see that counts governed their counties justly; he visited every part of his kingdom; he supervised the management of his huge estates.

SECTION 2
As You Read
Sample answer: Causes: People needed protection from invaders; kingdoms declined in power. Effects: Social classes well defined; manors were mostly self-sufficient.

Summary
1. Invasions by the Vikings, Muslims, and Magyars threatened them. There was no central government to protect them.
2. The three groups were those who fought (the nobles and knights), those who prayed (the officials of the Church), and those who worked (the peasants and serfs).
3. The peasants worked the land to grow food.

Graphic Organizer
Possible responses:
1. In exchange for military and other services, a lord (landowner) granted land to a vassal.
2. The same noble might be a vassal to several different lords.
3. There were three groups—those who fought, those who prayed, and those who worked. Social class was usually inherited.
4. In exchange for housing, land, and protection, serfs had to perform tasks to maintain the estate and to pay several different kinds of taxes.
5. The manor was practically self-sufficient, producing almost everything needed for daily life.
6. Acceptance was part of Church teachings; they believed that God decided people's social position.

SECTION 3

As You Read

Sample answer: Loyalty; Bravery; Courteousness; Protectiveness of the weak and poor; Piousness.

Summary

1. Knights fought on behalf of nobles for control of land.
2. *Possible response:* Serving under the lord of a castle, learning courtly manners, practicing fighting skills, serving under a knight.
3. Troubadours sang about the joys and sorrows of romantic love.
4. Women had little or no power in feudal society. But they played important roles in the lives of noble and peasant families.

Graphic Organizer

Possible responses:

1. at age seven, began training as a page in castle of another lord; at 14, began training as a squire, acting as servant to knight; at 21, became knight
2. saddles, stirrups, armor, high-flying missiles
3. fought in local wars or in tournaments
4. be loyal, brave, and courteous; defend three masters—feudal lord, God, and chosen lady; protect weak and poor
5. lived in and protected home of feudal lords, stone castles designed as fortresses with massive walls and guard towers
6. expected to defend his chosen lady and keep her entertained with love poems and songs

SECTION 4

As You Read

Sample answer: 1075: Lay investiture banned; 1077: Henry IV's journey to Canossa; 1122: The Concordat at Worms compromise on lay investiture; 1176: Battle of Legnano.

Summary

1. Two powerful punishments were excommunication (sending someone out of the Church and banning them from eternal salvation) and interdiction (forbidding all sacred actions from taking place in a certain area).
2. Henry IV wanted to regain his power after the pope had excommunicated him.
3. The Holy Roman Empire was broken up into feudal states and remained so during the Middle Ages.

Graphic Organizer

Possible responses:

1. Cause: Otto wants to limit power of nobles and form alliance with Church. Outcome: Pope crowns Otto emperor.
2. Cause: Pope resents control emperors had over clergy. Outcome: Henry IV calls a meeting of bishops and orders Gregory to step down from papacy.
3. Cause: Gregory excommunicates Henry, bishops and princes side with pope, and Henry wants pope's forgiveness. Outcome: Henry is forgiven, returns home, and punishes nobles.
4. Cause: Issue of lay investiture remains undecided. Outcome: Compromise is reached in which the emperor has veto power over appointment of a bishop, but only the Church can grant a bishop the symbols of Church office.
5. Cause: Frederick's brutality angers Italian merchants and the Church. Outcome: League soldiers defeat Frederick's feudal army; Frederick makes peace with pope.

The Formation of Western Europe

SECTION 1

As You Read

Sample answer: 910: Reforms begin; 1095: First Crusade; 1099: Christians capture Jerusalem; 1187: Jerusalem falls to Saladin; 1204: Christian Knights loot Constantinople; 1212: Children's Crusade; 1492: Reconquista ends in Spain.

Summary

1. Marriage of priests, the practice of simony, and appointment of bishops by kings

2. Gothic architecture was the new style. It soared upward and seemed to reach toward heaven.

3. Rulers and the Church favored the Crusades because they wanted Christians to gain control of the Holy Land. The people's support came from deep religious feelings.

4. The Reconquista, which took place in Spain, was the battle of the Christian rulers to take back land the Muslims had conquered in the 700s. By 1492, the last Muslim land fell.

5. Pope's power was cut, nobles' power reduced, trade with the East revived, and bitterness between Muslims and Christians

Graphic Organizer
Possible responses:

1. Reformers there had a desire to return to basic principles of Christianity.

2. The church had its own court, tax system, and diplomats.

3. The Church was wealthy; because cathedrals represented the City of God, they were glorious buildings, richly decorated.

4. The Muslims were threatening to conquer his capital of Constantinople.

5. The goal of this military expedition was to recover Jerusalem and the Holy Land from the Muslim Turks.

6. Many knights were fired by religious zeal. Others were looking for land, riches, and adventure. Kings and the Church saw the Crusades as an opportunity to get rid of quarrelsome knights who fought each other and who threatened the peace of the kingdom as well as Church property.

7. The states were carved out of land the Crusaders won—a narrow strip that stretched about 400 miles from Edessa in the north to Jerusalem in the south.

8. Saladin and Richard the Lion-hearted agreed to a truce in 1192.

9. Isabella and Ferdinand wanted to unify Spain under Christianity and to consolidate their own power.

10. The Crusades weakened the feudal nobility. Thousands of knights lost their lives and their fortunes in the Crusades.

SECTION 2
As You Read
Sample answer: Food supply increases; Guilds alter production; Trade expands; Banking and business practices change; Universities are created.

Summary

1. Students may name any three: climate warming, use of horses instead of oxen, a new harness that made the use of horses possible, and the three-field system.

2. The two kinds of guilds were merchant and craft.

3. Town fairs were held; merchants found ways to get money; Christians formed banks.

4. If peasants lived in the towns one year and one day, they became free.

5. The vernacular made literature available to those who could not read Latin. This was a much larger part of the population.

Graphic Organizer
Possible responses:

1. Horses gradually replaced oxen for plowing and for pulling wagons.

2. Food production, including sources of vegetable protein, increased resulting in an increase in population.

3. Guilds became powerful forces in medieval society.

4. More goods were available, new trade routes opened, and banking becomes an important business.

5. Towns grew and flourished.

6. People moved to towns to pursue the economic and social opportunities they offered.

7. These writers brought literature to many people, since most people could not read or understand Latin.

8. Universities, or groups of scholars and students, arose in western Europe.

9. Europeans acquired a huge new body of knowledge.

SECTION 3
As You Read
Sample answer: Step 1: Centralized government—policies applied to all; Step 2: Courts—Unified body of law or appeals; Step 3: Magna Carta—Guaranteed basic rights; Step 4—Parliament/Estates-General—included commoners in lawmaking.

Summary
1. The Vikings and the Anglo-Saxons invaded before the French.
2. The Magna Carta limited the power of the king. It protected the power of nobles. Later its protections were said to apply to all.
3. Philip II created a stronger central government. Louis IX set up royal courts.

Graphic Organizer
Possible responses:
1. English lords lost their land; William granted fiefs to Norman lords, who swore loyalty to him personally, thus laying foundation for centralized government.
2. sent royal judges to parts of England to collect taxes, settle lawsuits, and punish crimes; introduced use of the jury in English courts; laid foundation for English common law
3. By increasing the territory of France, he increased land under his own control and became more powerful than any of his vassals; he also established royal officials called bailiffs who presided over his courts and collected his taxes throughout France.
4. It guaranteed what are now seen as certain basic legal rights in both England and the United States. These guaranteed rights include no taxation without representation, a jury trial, and the protection of the law.
5. He created an appeals court, which could overturn decisions of local courts.
6. It was a legislative group composed of commoners—burgesses from every borough and knights from every county. Although under Edward I, Parliament was a royal tool that weakened the great lords,

as time went on it became strong enough to provide a check on royal power.

SECTION 4
As You Read
Sample answer: Split in Church—Cause: conflict between kings and pope; Effect: Church power weakened. Plague—Cause: epidemic from Asia; Effect: millions died, serfs freed, trade declined. Hundred Years' War—Cause: power struggles between French and English kings; Effect: English driven from European continent, rise of nationalism in both countries.

Summary
1. The Great Schism occurred when both the French and the Italians elected their own popes.
2. Students may name any three: the death of about one-third of the population of Europe, the decline of trade, inflation, smaller towns, peasant revolts, loss of Church prestige, persecution of Jews, and the end of the Middle Ages.
3. Joan of Arc led the French army to victory at Orléans.

Graphic Organizer
Possible responses:
1. in 1305, when the College of Cardinals chose a French pope who moved from Rome to Avignon
2. in 1417, when the Council of Constance elected a new pope to replace the three popes who had been forced to resign
3. weakened the church
4. in Asia, spread to Europe through trade
5. a severe decline in population and trade, higher prices, peasant revolts, and decline of the manorial system
6. When prayer and penances failed to stop the plague, the Church lost prestige.
7. English claims to the French throne
8. French eventually won and English left France except for port city of Calais
9. age of chivalry died and nationalism replaced feudal loyalties

Societies and Empires of Africa

SECTION 1
As You Read
Sample answer: Lineages share power, no centralized authority, elders negotiate conflict.

Summary
1. The Efe are hunter-gatherers. Women gather plant food. Men hunt animals.
2. Authority is spread over many lineages. This stops any one family from dominating.
3. The Berbers are North African Muslims who helped spread Islam in North Africa and to southern Spain.

Graphic Organizer
Possible responses:
1. semi-nomadic life, few possessions, distinctive hunting techniques
2. If conflicts cannot be settled by discussion, group members might move to a different band.
3. Systems of government have authority balanced among lineages of equal power; societies may be patrilineal or matrilineal; men usually hold positions of authority.
4. Young form close ties outside their lineage and are taught the duties and responsibilities required at different life stages.
5. Religious leaders are political rulers and obeying the law is a religious obligation.
6. helped bring order to states

SECTION 2
As You Read
Sample answer: Mali: Gold-salt trade, strict judicial system, built mosques. Songhai: Broke from Mali, had war canoes, horseback fighters, strong centralized government. Both: Controlled Timbuktu, strong leaders, created Muslim empires, dominated trade.

Summary
1. The two most important trade goods were gold and salt. Cloth and manufactured goods were also traded.

2. Mansa Musa made Mali twice the size of the old empire of Ghana. He named governors to head provinces and built mosques in two cities.
3. Songhai fell when it was defeated by a Moroccan army that used modern, more powerful weapons.
4. Benin was another West African kingdom that arose in the 1200s and reached its peak 100 years later.

Graphic Organizer
Possible responses:
1. (effect) Using camels, Berber nomads blazed new routes across the Sahara and trade increased.
2. (effect) With the source of its wealth gone, Ghana never regained power.
3. (cause) Gold was discovered farther east, causing a shift eastward in trade routes.
4. (cause) Most of Mansa Musa's successors did not govern well; also, new gold deposits were developed and trade shifted eastward again.
5. (cause) Unlike their foe, the Songhai warriors had no modern weapons.
6. (effect) These city-states became major centers for trade, profiting from supplying the needs of caravans.
7. (effect) This freed city-dwellers from farming; they could become craftspeople or traders.

SECTION 3
As You Read
Sample answer: Bantu & Arabs: Create Swahili. Muslims & East Africans: Bring Islam to East Africa. Portuguese & Mutapa: Ruler deposed.

Summary
1. Kilwa's location made it a thriving trading port. It was as far south on the coast as a ship from India could sail in one season. All trade goods from farther south had to come through Kilwa.
2. The Muslim slave trade involved about 1,000 slaves per year, who were sold into lives of household tasks in Arabia or Persia or as soldiers in India.

3. The people left Great Zimbabwe, although no one is sure why. They may have overused or destroyed their own grasslands, soil, or timber.

4. The rulers exchanged gold mined in nearby rivers and streams and by conquered peoples for luxury goods from coastal city-states.

Graphic Organizer
Possible responses:

1. Traders took advantage of the monsoons to sail across the Indian Ocean to East Africa.

2. It was as far south as a ship from India could sail and still sail home during the same monsoon season; trade goods from the south had to funnel into Kilwa so Asian merchants could buy them.

3. The Portuguese established themselves as a permanent presence on the East African coast.

4. Its area was good for farming and cattle raising; it was near an important trade route linking the inland gold fields with the coastal trading city of Sofala.

5. introduced Islamic religion and mosque architecture; exported enslaved Africans to India, China, Iraq, Persia, and Arabia

6. a. The original area had fertile soil, good rainfall, and ample wood—all important resources.

   b. Rulers conquered new land, including area along Zambezi River to the coast; they forced conquered people to pay tribute.

   c. Gold mining was widespread; conquered people worked in the mines.

   d. Portuguese were unable to conquer the empire.

People and Empires in the Americas

SECTION 1
As You Read

Sample answer: Northwest: Most important resource the Sea; Social classes based on wealth. Southwest: Hot and dry; Farming important; built pueblos. Both: High degree of social organization.

Summary

1. The Anasazi lived where the present-day states of Utah, Arizona, Colorado, and New Mexico meet. They built homes in the caves between the rocky walls of canyons. Later, they built pueblos by hand. Pueblos are large apartment-style homes made from stone and baked clay. The Mississippians lived in the woods east of the Mississippi River. They lived in villages such as Cahokia. In the center of Cahokia was a flat-topped pyramid with a temple at the top.

2. *Possible responses:* They were linked by trade; they believed the world was full of spirits and that people had to follow certain rituals and customs to live in peace; they shared respect for the land and did not believe in land ownership; they believed in the family as the most important social unit; they identified themselves with totems.

Graphic Organizer
Possible responses:

1. Environment: temperate Pacific Northwest, rich in resources
   Achievements: hunted whales in canoes; developed social classes, elaborate potlatch ceremony

2. Environment: Hohokam: Dry lands of what is now central Arizona; Anasazi: Dry lands of Four Corners area where present-day states of Utah, Arizona, Colorado, and New Mexico meet
   Achievements: used pottery, irrigation; built impressive cliff dwellings and villages with large apartment-style compounds of stone and sun-baked clay with just human labor

3. Environment: wooded lands east of the Mississippi River
   Achievements: built large burial mounds filled with finely crafted copper and stone objects; created prosperous villages based on trade and farming

4. Environment: wooded lands in present-day Northeastern U.S.
Achievements: developed varied cultures, formed political alliances such as the Iroquois League

Possible responses:
Political: Iroquois League
Economic: vast trading networks
Cultural: shared religious beliefs such as sacred spirits in nature, a supreme being, and respect for land as source of life; extended family (and sometimes clan) as a basis for social organization; use of totems as a symbol of clan or group unity

SECTION 2
As You Read
Sample answer: Urban centers; Religiosity; Calendars; Codices.

Summary
1. Each Maya city was independent and ruled by a god king. Each was a trade center as well as a religious center. The cities were large and were full of palaces, temples, and pyramids. There were at least 50 Maya cities, and they were linked by trade.
2. Maya writing was advanced. It was the most advanced writing system in the ancient Americas. It was used to record important historical events as well as the story of creation.
3. The decline may have resulted from war between city-states and an exodus to the jungle, or it may have resulted from overuse of the soil.

Graphic Organizer
Possible responses:
1. dry scrub forest of Yucatán, dense jungles of southeastern Mexico and northern Guatemala, highlands stretching from southern Mexico to El Salvador
2. city-states, each ruled by a god-king, comprised of central city with giant pyramids, temples, palaces, stone carvings, and surrounding residential

areas; served as center for religious ceremonies and trade
3. based on trade and farming; practiced sophisticated farming methods such as planting on raised platforms above swamps and on hillside terraces; grew maize, beans, and squash
4. three social classes—noble class consisting of priests and warriors; a middle class of merchants and artisans; and a lower class of peasants— headed by Maya king who was seen as a holy figure and whose position was hereditary
5. believed in many gods; prayed and offered gods food, blood, human sacrifice
6. developed calendar, math, astronomy, writing system

SECTION 3
As You Read
Sample answer: Teotihuacán; Toltec; nomadic Mexica; Tenochtitlán; Triple Alliance; Aztec Empire.

Summary
1. Teotihuacán was an early city-state in the Valley of Mexico that reached its peak around 500. It had as many as 200,000 people, many of whom were involved in the trade of obsidian.
2. The emperor was at the top. He was treated as both a god and a ruler. Military leaders, government officials, and priests were next highest. After that came commoners, merchants, craft workers, soldiers, and farmers who owned their land. At the bottom were slaves taken as captives in battle.
3. Aztecs sacrificed to the sun god because it was the most important of their gods. They believed that a sacrifice of human blood was necessary to make the god happy and make the sun rise every day. They sacrificed people taken captive in war.
4. Conquered people rebelled when the Aztecs wanted even more people to sacrifice.

Graphic Organizer

Possible responses:

1. For these poor nomads to succeed in their new environment, they had to adapt to the warlike ways of the city-states that governed the area.
2. They waged war to gain control over neighboring regions.
3. The Aztecs worshiped many gods; religion played a major role in Aztec society.
4. They needed to connect the island site of Tenochtitlán to the mainland.
5. The Aztecs believed that without regular offerings of blood, the sun god would not make the sun rise and all life would perish.
6. They needed a way to keep track of when they had to perform varied religious rituals and public ceremonies honoring the many gods.
7. The Aztecs had been demanding more and more tribute and sacrificial victims from the provinces under their control to meet the demands of Tenochtitlán's growing population.
8. He tried to reduce pressure on the provinces that had been forced to pay higher tributes.

SECTION 4

As You Read

Sample answer: Small administrative units; Roads; Mail system; Schooling; Trade; Official language; Taxation.

Summary

1. The Inca believed their ruler was related to the sun god. Only men from one of 11 noble families believed to be descendants of the sun god could serve as king.
2. Mita was an obligation to do labor for the state. It was required of all Incan subjects. It might take the form of work on state farms, roads, or buildings.
3. The empire was weakened by civil war, which enabled the Spaniards to conquer it.

Graphic Organizer

Possible responses:

1. The Inca built their empire on cultural foundations thousands of years old.

2. These traditions and beliefs helped to launch and unify the Incan Empire. One of these beliefs was that the Incan ruler was descended from the sun god, who would bring greatness to the empire.
3. A powerful and ambitious ruler, he quickly expanded the Incan Empire through conquests and diplomacy.
4. Conquered territories were divided into manageable community units governed by a central bureaucracy.
5. Quechua was imposed as the single official language for the varied peoples ruled by the Incas.
6. All cities built in conquered lands had the same government buildings.
7. A 14,000-mile-long network of bridges and roads, with all roads leading to the capital, tied the empire together.
8. The state controlled most economic activity and regulated the production and distribution of goods.
9. Religion reinforced the power of the state; Cuzco was both the administrative and religious capital of the empire.

European Renaissance and Reformation

SECTION 1

As You Read

Sample answer: I. Advantages: A. thriving cities, B. wealthy merchants, C. classical heritage. II. Values: A. citizens involved in politics, B. merchants dominated politics.

Summary

1. The Renaissance began in Italy because it had several important cities; these cities included a class of merchants and bankers; and artists were inspired by the classical ruins there.
2. Secular ideas are ideas centered on the things of the world.
3. Painting became more realistic as a result of the use of perspective; its subject changed to go beyond only the religious.

4. Renaissance writers wrote about their own thoughts and feelings; they also took a more detailed look at the individual.

Graphic Organizer

Possible responses:

1. Humanists influenced artists to carry on classical traditions and popularized the studies common to classical education.
2. Although people remained devoutly Catholic, the spirit of society was secular. Church leaders and the wealthy believed they could enjoy life without offending God.
3. They spent money to help artists and architects create works of genius.
4. They painted portraits of prominent citizens, showing what was distinctive about each; they glorified the human body in natural postures; they developed perspective to enhance realism.
5. They wrote in the vernacular; they wrote either for self-expression or to portray the individuality of their subjects.
6. Petrarch wrote sonnets about Laura, an ideal woman; Boccaccio wrote about the follies of his characters in the *Decameron,* and Machiavelli wrote about the imperfect conduct of humans in *The Prince.*

SECTION 2
As You Read
Sample answer: about 1440: Gutenberg invents printing press; 1450s: Northern Renaissance begins; 1509: Erasmus writes *The Praise of Folly*; 1516: More writes *Utopia*; mid-1500s: Elizabethan Age begins; late 1500s: Shakespeare writes plays and poems.

Summary
1. In northern Europe, Renaissance thinkers combined classical learning with religious thinking.
2. Northern European artists showed their own lives and times in realistic ways. They often painted lifelike portraits and scenes of peasant life.
3. The most famous writer was Shakespeare. Also famous was Thomas More.

4. People read more. They also began to read the Bible on their own, which led to their forming their own ideas about Christianity.

Graphic Organizer
Possible responses:
1. Population began to recover from the Plague; the Hundred Years' War ended, cities grew rapidly, city merchants became wealthy enough to sponsor artists.
2. Books were cheap so many people could buy them; books were written in the vernacular for people who had not had classical educations; because books were more readily available, more people learned to read.

Possible responses:
3. Produced woodcuts and engravings whose realism influenced other artists; his work shows not only religious subjects (which were also subjects of art in middle ages), but also classical myths and realistic landscapes.
4. Van Eyck used oil-based paints to develop new techniques. He applied many layers of paint to create a variety of subtle colors in clothing and jewels. Oil painting became popular and spread to Italy. Realistic details showed the personalities of people he painted.
5. interested in realistic details and individuals; painted scenes from everyday life; produced paintings that illustrated proverbs, taught a moral, or protested Spanish rule over his country
6. Erasmus was a Christian humanist writer whose book *The Praise of Folly* poked fun at flaws in real people, such as greedy merchants, pompous priests, and the like. He believed that to improve society, people should study the Bible; he also believed in Christianity of the heart, not in a religion of rules and ceremonies.
7. More was concerned with society's flaws. In his book *Utopia,* he tried to show an ideal model of society.
8. His plays examine human flaws and also express the Renaissance's high view of

human nature. He drew on Greek and Roman classics for some of his plots.

SECTION 3
As You Read
Sample answer: 1. Luther excommunicated. 2. Peasants revolt. 3. Lutheran Church founded.

Summary
1. Church critics wanted popes to be less concerned with luxury and political power. They did not want to pay taxes to the Church in Rome. They wanted the Church to become more spiritual and humble.
2. *Possible response:* Martin Luther began the Reformation by challenging Church practices.
3. *Possible response:* Luther's protest allowed people to criticize not only the Church but emperors, too.
4. Henry VIII had Parliament pass laws to remove England from the Catholic Church. This action started the Church of England.

Graphic Organizer
Possible responses:
1. [causes] He attacked Tetzel's selling of indulgences. [effects] Luther's words were spread all over Germany and attracted many followers.
2. [causes] The pope realized that Luther was a serious threat to papal authority. The emperor, a devout Catholic, also felt threatened. [effects] Luther was sheltered in Saxony, where he translated the New Testament into German. When he returned to Wittenberg, he found many of his ideas already in use. He and his followers had become a separate religious group called Lutherans.
3. [causes] They were excited by talk of Christian freedom and applied this idea to social freedom by demanding an end to serfdom. [effects] When the armies of the German princes (at Luther's request) crushed the revolt, killing thousands of people, many peasants rejected Luther's religious leadership.

4. [causes] The Holy Roman Emperor had fought a war against the German Protestant princes and defeated them. However, he couldn't force them back into the Catholic Church. [effects] The settlement ended the war and allowed the ruler of each German state to decide his state's religion.
5. [causes] Henry VIII needed to annul his marriage to Catherine and remarry in order to have a male heir. When the pope would not agree to this, Henry called a Reformation Parliament to strip away the pope's power in England. The Act of Supremacy completed Henry's break with the pope by making the king the head of England's church. [effects] Henry closed all English monasteries and seized their wealth and land. This act increased royal power as well as the king's treasury.
6. [causes] Elizabeth returned England from Catholicism (under Queen Mary) to Protestantism and asked Parliament to set up a national church. [effects] The Anglican Church became the only legal church in England and people were required to attend its services. Elizabeth organized the church so that both Catholic moderates and Protestant moderates might accept it.

SECTION 4
As You Read
Sample answer: Zwingli attacked abuses in Church; Calvin built on Luther's ideas, developed idea of predestination, and led a theocracy; Catholic reformers improved unity within Catholic Church and established high-quality education.

Summary
1. Calvinism is a body of religious teachings based on John Calvin's ideas, which included predestination.
2. Two women who played important roles in the Reformation were Margaret of Navarre and Katherina von Bora.
3. The Church passed doctrines saying that the Church's interpretation of the Bible

was final; that Christians needed to do good works to win salvation; that the Bible and Church had equal authority; and that indulgences were valid expressions of faith.

4. The rise in power of individual monarchs and states and the eventual development of the modern nation-state

Graphic Organizer
Possible responses:
1. People are sinful by nature; only the elect are saved; doctrine of predestination states that God has always known who the elect are; government should be in the hands of religious leaders; morality should be rigidly regulated.
2. Presbyterianism was based on Calvinist ideas; each community church was governed by presbyters.
3. Only adults could decide to be baptized; church and state should be separate; Anabaptists refused to fight in wars; they shared possessions.
4. They founded and staffed schools throughout Europe, sent out missionaries to convert non-Christians to Catholicism, and sought to stop Protestantism from spreading.
5. They sent missionaries to all the continents and founded schools, colleges, and universities throughout the world.
6. Pope Paul III had a council of cardinals investigate abuses within the Church; he approved the Jesuit order; he used the Inquisition to identify and punish heresy in papal territories; he convened the Council of Trent during which church leaders agreed on several doctrines. Pope Paul IV carried out the council's decrees, had the council draw up an Index of Forbidden Books, and had the offensive books collected and burned.
7. As Protestant churches flourished, religion no longer united Europe; as the Church's power declined, kings and states gained power, paving the way for nation-states; as Church authority was successfully questioned, groundwork was laid for

rejection of Christian belief that occurred in Western culture in later centuries.

The Muslim World Expands

SECTION 1
As You Read
Sample answer: Osman: Established Muslim state in Anatolia. Orkhan I: Captured Adrianople. Mehmed I: Defeated his brothers. Murad II: Invaded Europe.

Summary
1. The Ottomans were the followers of Osman, the ghazi who built a small kingdom in Anatolia.
2. Mehmed II was a sultan who helped bring the Ottoman Empire to its greatest power and who captured Constantinople in 1453.
3. *Possible responses:* Two of Suleyman's accomplishments were bringing the empire to its greatest size and revising the laws of the empire.

Graphic Organizer
Possible responses:
1. built a small state in Anatolia between 1300 and 1326 to begin the rule of the Ottomans
2. restored power of Ottoman military and began expanding the Ottoman Empire; defeated Venetians, invaded Hungary, and overcame Italian crusaders in Balkans
3. conquered Constantinople in dramatic fashion, opening ship traffic between Ottomans' territories in Asia and in the Balkans; opened Constantinople to citizens of many religions, who rebuilt the city
4. defeated Safavids of Persia, then conquered Syria, Palestine, the Islam holy cities of Mecca and Medina, and Egypt, ending the Egyptian Mameluke Dynasty and making the once-powerful Egypt just another province of the growing Ottoman Empire
5. captured Rhodes, gaining control of the eastern Mediterranean; conquered peoples

of the North African coastline, controlling trade routes to the interior

Possible responses:
Social: bound Ottoman Empire together into workable social structure, established efficient government organization and palace bureaucracy staffed by janissaries, simplified system of taxation, revamped the laws of the empire
Cultural: built Mosque of Suleyman, encouraged learning, supported art and literature

SECTION 2
As You Read
Sample answer: Copied the Ottoman style of military; Used Chinese artisans' work in buildings; Blended designs into carpets.

Summary
1. Four causes of cultural blending are migration, trade, conquest, pursuit of religious freedom, or conversion.
2. When in power, the Sunni killed Shi'a. When Shi'a were in power, they killed Sunni.
3. *Possible answers:* Shah Abbas gave new weapons to the army to make them better fighters, got rid of corrupt officials, brought gifted artists to his empire, and drew on good ideas from other cultures.
4. Shah Abbas killed his most able sons, leaving weak, ineffective grandsons.

Graphic Organizer
Possible responses:
1. migration, trade, conquest, religious conversion or religious freedom
2. all of those except for migration
3. led military to victories that seized most of what is now Iran, took the ancient Persian title of shah, and established Shi'a Islam as the state religion
4. became a religious tyrant who put to death all who did not convert to Shi'ism; caused conflict between Shi'a and Sunni Muslims that continues today

5. established relations with Europe, invited Chinese artisans to empire, based government on Ottoman model
6. a demand for Persian carpets that helped change carpet weaving from a local craft to a national industry

SECTION 3
As You Read
Sample answer: 1494: Babur; early 1500s: Humayun; 1556: Akbar; 1605: Jahangir (and Nur Jahan); early 1600s: Shah Jahan; 1658: Aurangzeb.

Summary
1. Babur was the founder of the Mughal empire.
2. Hired both Hindus and Muslims; ended taxes on pilgrims; had fair taxes
3. Harshly. He punished Hindus and destroyed their temples.
4. *Possible answer:* The empire began to decline. There were internal difficulties with both Sikhs and Hindus.

Graphic Organizer
Possible responses:
1. gains control of part of India and lays foundation for Mughal Empire
2. contributes to the quality of government
3. prevents creation of a feudal aristocracy but discourages Mughal officials from developing their lands
4. turns potential enemies into supporters and helps him unify a land of at least 100 million people
5. Arts, architecture, and Hindu literature flourish; a new language, Urdu, is created.
6. creates a bitter and ongoing religious conflict between Sikhs and Mughals
7. depletes empire's resources; people heavily taxed and denied important tools and services
8. Hindu Rajputs rebel, Marathas found their own state, and Sikhs begin a state in the Punjab.
9. His sons fight wars of succession, further weakening the empire and enhancing power of local lords.

Guided Reading Workbooks Answer Key

An Age of Exploration and Isolation

SECTION 1

As You Read

Sample answer: 1419: Prince Henry founds navigation school; 1487: Dias sails around tip of Africa; 1498: Da Gama reaches Calicut; 1511: Portuguese gain control of Strait of Malacca.

Summary

1. The two reasons were the desire for wealth and the desire to spread Christianity.
2. Spain and Portugal made the Treaty of Tordesillas, which split the lands between them.
3. The Dutch and English set up East India Companies to control and defend their trade.

Graphic Organizer

Possible responses:

1. caravel with its triangular sails that allowed it to sail against the wind, astrolabe, magnetic compass
2. immediate: increased tensions between Spain and Portugal long term: opened up the Americas to European colonization
3. By agreeing to honor the Line of Demarcation that divided Portuguese and Spanish land claims, the countries opened the era of exploration and colonization in earnest.
4. gained a direct sea route to Asia
5. to end Portuguese domination of Asian trade and establish its own trade empire there
6. became a great naval power, allied with England to break Portuguese control of trade, and then drove English out of region
7. Until the Europeans began to conquer the region, the peoples of Asia remained relatively unaffected by European contact.

SECTION 2

As You Read

Sample answer: Hongwu: defeated Mongols; ruled 1368–1398; first Ming emperor; encouraged agriculture, Confucian standards, administrative reforms; became brutal. Yonglo: 1398, assumed throne; moved capital to Beijing; built Forbidden City; sponsored first Aheng He voyage; increased tributaries. Kangxi: ruled 1661–1722; first Manchu emperor; lowered taxes; defeated Mongols; patronized arts. Qian-long: 1736–1795; hard-working; dealt with border unrest and Europeans.

Summary

1. *Possible response:* China learned foreign ideas by means of its expeditions. It was affected by those who wanted its silk and ceramics and would pay silver for them. It was also affected by missionaries.
2. *Possible response:* The Chinese insisted that Europeans had to follow certain rules to continue trading with them. Only the Dutch were willing to do so.
3. Agriculture improved, nutrition improved, and the population grew. Women continued to have few rights.

Graphic Organizer

Possible responses:

1. reformed agriculture, restored civil service and Confucian moral standards
2. increased rice production, improved irrigation, introduced fish farming and commercial crops
3. to keep the influence of outsiders to a minimum
4. led to smuggling, increase in commerce and manufacturing, introduction of Christianity and European inventions
5. by preserving Chinese traditions and Confucian beliefs and restoring prosperity and safety
6. Art reflected technical skills, rather than creativity; plays depicted Chinese history and heroes.
7. restricted trading to special ports and demanded tribute and "kowtow" rituals
8. The Dutch followed Chinese rules while the British refused to kowtow.

SECTION 3
As You Read
Sample answer: Oda Mobunaga: 1568 took Kyoto, defeated enemy daimyo; 1575 used firearms in battle. Hideyoshi: 1590 claimed most of Japan; 1592 invaded Korea. Ieyasu: 1600 defeated rivals; 1603 took shogun title; moved capital to Edo; restricted daimyo power; rule of law.

Summary
1. Oda Nobunaga, Toyotomi Hideyoshi, and Tokugawa Ieyasu helped bring Japan under one rule.
2. Old culture included ceremonial dramas, stories of ancient warriors, and paintings of classical scenes. New culture included kabuki theater, woodblock prints of city life, and haiku.
3. Tokugawa worried about the loss of traditional Japanese beliefs. He wanted to keep Christianity and other foreign ideas out of Japan.

Graphic Organizer
Possible responses:
1. These feudal lords fought each other for over a century, but eventually one was victorious, Tokugawa Ieyasu, and unified Japan.
2. seized imperial capital and set out on a mission to eliminate rivals for power
3. continued Nobunaga's mission by combining brute force with political alliances, gained control over most of the country
4. defeated rivals, completed unification, and founded Tokugawa Shogunate
5. brought about more than two centuries of stability, prosperity, and isolation
6. introduced many unfamiliar items from Europe, including firearms which in turn changed samurai traditions and led to fortification of castles and eventually, the growth of cities and towns
7. at first, Japanese converts to Christianity; later, religious persecution and eventually the end of Christianity in Japan
8. allowed the Tokugawa shoguns to monopolize profitable foreign trade; made Japan self-sufficient and closed to European influences

The Atlantic World
SECTION 1
As You Read
Sample answer: Columbus's arrival; Cortés defeats the Aztecs; Pizarro conquers the Inca; conquistadors colonize the southwest United States.

Summary
1. The voyages of Columbus, Vespucci, Balboa, and Magellan provided new knowledge.
2. The main goal of Cortés was great wealth, such as gold and silver.
3. Hernando Cortés conquered the Aztec Empire, and Francisco Pizarro conquered the Inca Empire.
4. Coronado led an expedition into land that is now part of the United States.
5. Priests and others criticized the *encomienda* system. Many Native Americans resisted or rebelled against Spanish rule.

Graphic Organizer
Possible responses:
1. The voyages began the process of European colonization of the Americas.
2. They became the first to sail around the world.
3. superior weaponry; aid of some groups of natives; European diseases that killed many Native Americans, who had no immunity to them
4. They created a large mestizo population, imposed their culture, and exploited Native Americans as laborers.
5. Mainly priests explored and colonized much of the region.
6. replacement of Native American forced labor with African forced labor, enslavement of Africans

SECTION 2

As You Read

Sample answer: New France: St. Lawrence and Mississippi Rivers, fur trade, New Netherland: Hudson River and Hudson Bay, fur trade. Massachusetts Bay: Coastal Massachusetts, religious freedom.

Summary

1. Trade in beaver fur was the main activity.
2. English colonists first settled in what is now Virginia and Massachusetts.
3. England fought the French and Indian War with France. At the end of this war, France was forced to give up all its land in North America.
4. The English colonists, in particular, wanted to farm and settle the land that the Native Americans used to hunt or to grow their food. The Native Americans also suffered from war and disease.

Graphic Organizer

Possible responses:

1. Giovanni da Verrazzano, Jacques Cartier, Samuel de Champlain, Marquette and Joliet; find a sea route to the Pacific, establish fur trade
2. London investors who received a charter from King James to found a colony; England's first permanent North American colony
3. Pilgrims, Puritans; search for religious freedom
4. land along Hudson River, Hudson Bay, and Hudson Strait; expand fur trade, set up permanent colonies

SECTION 3

As You Read

Sample answer: In Africa: Loss of population, families torn apart, and cultures lost. In the Americas: Slave traders benefited, slave owners benefited, enslaved Africans forced to adapt to brutal conditions, African cultures spread.

Summary

1. African slaves were brought to the Americas when Native American workers began dying from disease and warfare. They were brought to work on the large plantations.
2. They captured Africans inland and then delivered them to the coast for guns and other goods.
3. The triangular trade was trade between Europe, the Americas, and Africa. It brought manufactured goods to Africa, slaves to the Americas, and various American items from the West Indies to North America or from North America to Europe.
4. African labor contributed to the economic development of the Americas. Africans also brought their culture with them, including their art, music, and food. These influenced American society.

Graphic Organizer

Possible responses:

1. At first, colonists forced Native Americans to work their profitable mines and plantations. But as Native Americans began dying by the millions, the colonists bought Africans to replace Native American workers.
2. Demand for slaves grew massively as Brazil's sugar industry expanded.
3. Some African rulers helped deliver slaves to Europeans in exchange for goods.
4. They bought and sold slaves. When some African rulers opposed the slave trade, merchants developed new trade routes.
5. population drain, introduction of guns that helped spread war and devastation
6. separation from families, harsh lives, eventual development of rich cultural heritage
7. economic and cultural development, back-breaking labor and farming expertise that helped many colonies survive
8. addition of Africans to population group, mixed-race populations, cultural additions, cultural blending

SECTION 4
As You Read
Sample answer: Potato, Americas, nourished millions; Horse, Europe, transformed transportation; Smallpox, Europe, killed millions.

Summary
1. *Possible response:* Agricultural products, including tomatoes, squash, tobacco, peanuts, potatoes, and corn, were taken from the Americas. Different agricultural products, including citrus fruits and bananas, were brought back.
2. An economic system based on private ownership of property and the right to earn a profit.
3. *Possible response:* The colonies provided goods that could be sold in trade; they helped create a favorable balance of trade for the Europeans.

Graphic Organizer
Possible responses:
1. Causes: colonization of Americas
   Effects: introduction of new products and new diseases, changes in diet, death of millions of Native Americans
2. Causes: establishment of colonial empires, expansion of overseas trade, increased wealth for many individuals and countries
   Effects: rise of capitalism, rise of merchant class, growth of towns
3. Causes: increased money supply, increased demand for goods
   Effects: scarcity of goods, rising prices
4. Causes: high cost of colonization, need to reduce potential losses
   Effects: establishment of Jamestown and other colonies in North America
5. Causes: desire for power, wealth, self-sufficiency
   Effects: creation of colonial empires

Absolute Monarchs in Europe
SECTION 1
As You Read
Sample answer: Conditions: Decline of feudalism; Colonial wealth; Religious conflicts; Territorial conflicts.

Summary
1. Philip II was the ruler of Spain and its colonies who increased his power by taking control of Portugal.
2. El Greco, Diego Velásquez, Miguel de Cervantes
3. Possible response: Problems, such as unfair taxes and rising prices of goods, weakened Spain's economy and power. Spain also lost power as it lost provinces.
4. The Dutch had the largest fleet of merchant ships in the world and the most important bankers in Europe.
5. Absolute rulers believed in holding all power and in their divine right to rule.

Graphic Organizer
Possible responses:
1. Spain built a powerful army and navy, and its monarchs and nobles became patrons of artists, leading to a golden age in the arts.
2. As the population grew, people demanded more food and other goods, so merchants were able to raise prices. As silver bullion flooded the market, its value dropped and it took more to buy anything.
3. severe inflation, lack of a middle class, expulsion of Jews and Muslims, outdated manufacturing methods, and the high cost of wars
4. The Dutch rebelled and eventually the largely Protestant northern provinces of the Netherlands united and declared independence from Spain.
5. stable government, strong middle class, large naval fleet, mighty trading empire
6. decline of feudalism, rise of cities, creation of a middle class, and growth of national kingdoms

SECTION 2
As You Read
Sample answer: 1643: Louis XIV becomes king; 1648–1653: Anti-Mazarin riots; 1661: Cardinal Mazarin dies, Louis takes control; 1672: Louis invades Dutch Netherlands; 1685: Louis cancels the Edict of Nantes; 1701–1714: the War of the Spanish Succession; 1715: Louis dies.

Summary
1. Cardinal Richelieu increased the power of the crown and decreased the power of the nobles.
2. Louis XIV kept the nobles out of his government and gave more power to the government officials who reported to him.
3. Louis XIV spent too much money on wars and, along with Spain, lost land after the War of the Spanish Succession.

Graphic Organizer
Possible responses:
1. converted to Catholicism and issued Edict of Nantes, which declared that Huguenots could live in peace in France and set up their own houses of worship in certain cities; devoted his reign to rebuilding France and its prosperity
2. forbade Protestant cities from having walls; weakened power of nobles by ordering them to take down their fortified castles and by increasing power of government agents
3. turned them to skepticism, the idea that nothing can be known for certain, and led them to question church doctrine, which claimed to be the only truth
4. followed a strict policy of mercantilism by taking steps to make France self-sufficient, expanding and protecting French industries, and encouraging migration to France's colony of Canada, where the fur trade would add to French commercial strength
5. popularized opera and ballet, supported writers such as Molière, promoted art that glorified the monarchy and supported absolute rule

6. His many enemies combined forces in the League of Augsburg and thereby became strong enough to stop France.
7. made France a power in Europe and a model of culture, but laid the groundwork for revolution because of staggering debts and royal abuse of power

SECTION 3
As You Read
Sample answer: Maria Theresa: Decreased power of nobility; fought Prussia; allied with France; limited forced labor of peasants. Frederick: Fought Austria; allied with Britain; encouraged religious toleration and legal reform.

Summary
1. *Possible response:* The Thirty Years' War weakened the power of Austria and Spain, made France stronger, caused great suffering in Germany, ended religious wars in Europe, and gave all countries equal power to negotiate with the others.
2. The Hapsburgs were the ruling family of Austria, Hungary, and Bohemia.
3. Britain gained economic domination of India.

Graphic Organizer
Possible responses:
1. Responses may cite the tension between Catholic and Lutheran princes in Germany, their fear of the spread of Calvinism, and Ferdinand's attempt to limit Protestantism and then to crush a Protestant revolt in Bohemia.
2. Responses may mention that it devastated Germany so that it did not become a unified state until the 1800s; weakened the Hapsburg states of Spain and Austria; strengthened France, which received German territory; ended religious wars in Europe; and marked the beginning of the modern state system.
3. The economy of western Europe was commercial and capitalistic while that of central Europe remained feudal, dependent on serf labor, and untouched by the commercial revolution.

4. Strong landowning nobles hindered the development of strong monarchy. The Thirty Years' War had weakened the Holy Roman Empire.

5. Responses may mention that during the Thirty Years' War, they reconquered Bohemia, wiped out Protestantism there, and created a loyal Czech nobility. After the war, they centralized the government and created a standing army.

6. Responses may mention that they created a strong standing army; created a military state and bought the loyalty of the Junkers by giving the landowning nobility the exclusive right to be officers in the army; weakened representative assemblies; and took over Silesia.

life; imposed heavy taxes to pay for his huge, improved army

5. introduced potatoes, which became staple of Russian diet; started first Russian newspaper; ordered nobles to adopt Western fashions; raised status of women by having them attend social gatherings; advanced education by opening schools and ordering some to leave Russia to study

6. went to war against Sweden to gain a port on the Baltic Coast

7. forced thousands of serfs to work on building St. Petersburg on unhealthy swampy land

8. ordered many Russian nobles to leave Moscow and settle in the new port city capital

SECTION 4
As You Read
Sample answer: Visited western Europe; Built St. Petersburg; Brought the Orthodox Church under state control; Reduced power of the nobles; Promoted men from lower ranks; Modernized the army; Opened schools; Promoted Western ideas.

Summary
1. Ivan the Terrible added lands to Russia and gave the country a code of laws. He also used secret police to hunt down enemies and kill them.
2. Peter the Great traveled to Europe to learn about new technology and ways of working.
3. Peter the Great increased his own power by putting the Church under his control and cutting the power of the nobles.

Graphic Organizer
Possible responses:
1. increased powers as absolute ruler
2. replaced patriarch with Holy Synod to run Church under his direction
3. recruited able men from lower-ranking families, gave them positions of authority, and rewarded them with land grants, making them loyal to him alone
4. expanded army and hired European officers to train soldiers who served for

SECTION 5
As You Read
Sample answer: James I: Money and reform of the English church; Charles I: Money, rule of law, and Anglican ritual; James II: Appointment of Catholic officials.

Summary
1. Charles I dissolved Parliament and went directly against the Petition of Right.
2. Charles I was executed, and Puritan leader Oliver Cromwell assumed power.
3. The Glorious Revolution took place to remove the Catholic king, James II, from the throne and to place the Protestant king and queen, William and Mary, on the throne.
4. The development of the constitutional monarchy, the Bill of Rights, and the establishment of a cabinet all gave Parliament more power.

Graphic Organizer
Possible responses:
1. struggled with Parliament over money; offended Puritan members of Parliament by refusing to make Puritan reforms
2. Struggles over money led to forced signing of Petition of Right, dissolution of Parliament, passage of laws limiting royal power, effort to arrest leaders of

Parliament, and finally the English Civil War.

3. Cromwell abolished the monarchy and the House of Lords; later he sent the remaining members of Parliament home and ruled as a dictator.

4. Parliament invited Charles II to rule and passed *habeas corpus,* which limited king's power to jail opponents.

5. fought over appointment of Catholics to high office in violation of English law

6. governed as partners, with power of monarchy limited by Bill of Rights

Enlightenment and Revolution

SECTION 1

As You Read

Sample answer: Renaissance inspires new curiosity; Exploration broadens European horizons; Scientific discoveries challenge accepted thinking; Printing press spreads ideas.

Summary

1. The Scientific Revolution was a new way of thinking about the natural world based on careful observation and a willingness to question old ideas.

2. The new discoveries destroyed the idea that the earth was at the center of the universe.

3. Both Francis Bacon and René Descartes helped advance the use of the scientific method.

4. Scientists learned more about the human body and the circulation of blood. They also learned about vaccination.

Graphic Organizer

Possible responses:

1. Renaissance inspired spirit of curiosity; discoveries of classical manuscripts led to realization that ancient scholars often did not agree; scholars began to question ideas that had been accepted for hundreds of years; printing press spread new ideas quickly.

2. Long sea voyages required better navigational instruments, which led to research in astronomy and mathematics. As scientists looked more closely at the world around them, they made discoveries that did not match ancient beliefs.

3. Planets revolve around the sun.

4. Mathematical laws govern planetary motion; orbits of the planets are elliptical, not circular.

5. Each pendulum swing takes the same amount of time; falling objects accelerate at a fixed rate; Jupiter has moons.

6. The same force—gravity—rules all matter on earth and in space. Every object in the universe attracts every other; the degree of attraction is determined by mass and distance.

7. invention of telescope, microscope, barometer, thermometer

8. study of human anatomy, first vaccine (against smallpox)

9. Boyle's law explaining relationship of volume, temperature, and pressure of gas; discovery of oxygen

SECTION 2

As You Read

Sample answer: I. A. Hobbes's social contract, B. Locke's natural rights. II. A. Reason supports all, B. Philosophes support tolerance, separation of powers, freedoms, humanity. III. A. Women want education and equality, B. Women spread Enlightenment ideas. IV. A. Belief in progress, B. More secular outlook, C. Importance of individual.

Summary

1. Hobbes believed people had to give up their rights and obey a strong king. Locke felt people had natural rights, and it was the job of government to protect those rights.

2. The types of freedoms included freedom of religious belief, freedom of speech, political freedom, and human freedom.

3. *Possible response:* Enlightenment ideas helped create revolution, spread the idea of progress, create the hope of improving

society, make the world less spiritual, and make the individual more important.

Graphic Organizer
Possible responses:
1. believed in tolerance, reason, and freedom of thought, expression, and religious belief; fought against prejudice and superstition
2. advocated separation of powers and checks and balances to keep any individual or group from gaining complete control of government
3. committed to individual freedom; viewed government as an agreement among free individuals to create a society guided by the "general will"; unlike other Enlightenment thinkers, believed that civilization corrupted people's natural goodness and destroyed freedom and equality
4. believed laws existed to preserve social order; advocated a criminal justice system based on fairness and reason
5. believed that women, like men, need education to become virtuous and useful; argued for women's rights to become educated and to participate in politics

SECTION 3
As You Read
Sample answer: Ideas: Encyclopedia, salon. Art/Literature: Neoclassicism, novels, classical music. Monarchy: Frederick II, "servant of state; Joseph II, abolished serfdom.

Summary
1. Salons were important because artists and thinkers met there and exchanged their ideas.
2. Possible response: The neoclassical style appeared in art; new forms developed in music; and the novel became popular in literature.
3. Frederick the Great was typical of enlightened despots because he made some changes that helped people, but he did not end serfdom.

Graphic Organizer
Possible responses:
1. spread enlightened thinking in all areas by publishing the *Encyclopedia*
2. broke from traditionally ornate musical forms and developed the sonata and symphony
3. set a new standard for elegance and originality with his varied and numerous musical compositions
4. exhibited great range in his works; moved from the classical style of Mozart to begin new trend that carried music into the Age of Romanticism
5. wrote *Pamela*, the first English novel
6. committed himself to the goal of reforming and strengthening his country; granted many religious freedoms, reduced censorship, improved education and the justice system, and abolished torture; considered that the king should be "first servant of the state"
7. abolished serfdom, initiated legal reforms, introduced freedom of the press, supported freedom of religion
8. tried to modernize and reform Russia according to the writings of the philosophes; accomplished limited reforms

SECTION 4
As You Read
Sample answer: Stamp Act/Protest; Tea tax/Boston Tea Party; Weak Articles of Confederation/ Constitutional Convention; Mistrust of central government/Federal system.

Summary
1. The colonists thought of themselves less and less as British subjects, yet they were subjects, and Britain tried to control them.
2. *Possible response:* The revolution began with taxes and boycotts; it continued with shooting, the formation of an army, and the issuance of the Declaration of Independence.
3. The Constitution divides power between the three branches of government and also

between the states and the federal government.

Graphic Organizer

Possible responses:

1. Cause: need to pay off debts from French and Indian War
   Effect: Colonists boycott British manufactured goods in protest; Parliament repeals Stamp Act tax.
2. Cause: Colonists protest an import tax on tea and dump tea off British ships.
   Effect: First Continental Congress meets to protest punishment of Boston.
3. Cause: British soldiers and American militiamen exchange fire at Lexington and Concord.
   Effect: American Revolution begins.
4. Cause: France wants to weaken its enemy Britain.
   Effect: Combined forces result in victory for the Americans.
5. Cause: States need a plan for a national government but want to protect their own authority.
   Effect: National government is set up but is powerless to govern.

The French Revolution and Napoleon

SECTION 1
As You Read
Sample answer: Rising debt; New taxes; Weak leadership; Rise in bread prices.

Summary
1. First Estate—the Roman Catholic clergy; Second Estate—the nobles; Third Estate—merchants and skilled workers, city workers, peasants.
2. The spread of Enlightenment ideas, problems in the economy, and a weak king and unpopular queen
3. After the delegates of Third Estate argued about their unfair share of votes in the Estates-General, they formed the National Assembly to represent all the French people.

4. During the Great Fear, peasants destroyed nobles' homes and legal papers. A mob of women, angry about high bread prices, marched to Versailles and forced the king and queen to move to Paris.

Graphic Organizer

Possible responses:

1. The First Estate and Second Estate had privileges not granted to the Third Estate, to which about 97 percent of the people belonged. Heavily taxed and discontented, the Third Estate was eager for change.
2. People of the Third Estate began questioning long-standing ideas about government and spoke of equality and liberty.
3. A heavy tax burden, high prices, food shortages, and extravagant spending by the king and queen fueled discontent.
4. An indecisive king put off dealing with the crisis until it was too late.
5. Delegates of the Third Estate refused to be dominated by the clergy and nobles and asserted their independence.
6. It marked the end of absolute monarchy and the beginning of representative government.
7. In response, the king yielded to the demands of the National Assembly.
8. The fall of the Bastille into the control of French common people became a symbolic act of revolution.

SECTION 2
As You Read
Sample answer: War with Prussia and Austria; Monarchy abolished; Reign of Terror; Directory governs.

Summary
1. New laws ended special rights for members of the First and Second Estates, gave equal rights to all French men, and decreased the power of the Catholic Church.
2. The émigrés wanted to end revolutionary changes and bring back the old government; the sans-culottes wanted even

more revolutionary changes and greater
political power.
3. The king lost his powers, was declared a
common citizen, was tried and convicted
for treason, and then beheaded.
4. The Reign of Terror led to Robespierre's
own beheading and to a new, less
revolutionary plan of government.

Graphic Organizer
Possible responses:
1. liberty, property, security, resistance to
oppression, equal justice, freedom of
speech, freedom of religion
2. Many were conservative Catholics who
were offended by attempts to make the
church a part of the state.
3. radicals, moderates, conservatives
4. that the revolution would spread beyond
France and affect their countries
5. The Legislative Assembly gave up the
idea of a limited monarchy, deposed the
king, and called for the election of a new
legislature to replace itself.
6. to build a "republic of virtue"
7. People of all classes grew weary of the
Terror and shifted from radical left to
conservative right.

SECTION 3
As You Read
Sample answer: 1795: Napoleon defends
against royalists; 1796: Victories in Italy;
1799: Coup brings him to power; 1800:
Plebiscite gives him total power.

Summary
1. Napoleon seized power in a coup d'état.
2. Napoleon improved tax collection,
removed dishonest government workers,
started new public schools for ordinary
citizens, returned some power to the
church, and wrote a new set of laws—the
Napoleonic Code.
3. Napoleon added the Austrian Netherlands,
parts of Italy, and Switzerland. He gave up
land in the New World and lost a key
battle with Britain.

Graphic Organizer
Possible responses:
1. Goal(s): Stable economy and more
equality in taxation
Result(s): Steady supply of tax money,
better control of economy, financial
management
2. Goal(s): Comprehensive and uniform
system of laws
Result(s): Elimination of many injustices;
promotion of order over individual rights,
which were restricted
3. Goal(s): Regaining French control;
restoring productive sugar industry
Result(s): Failure; death of thousands of
soldiers
4. Goal(s): Make money; cut losses in
Americas; punish British
Result(s): Assured power of U.S.; gave
England a powerful rival
5. Goal(s): Remove threat of British navy;
defeat major enemy
Result(s): Assured supremacy of British
navy; forced Napoleon to give up plans to
invade Britain

SECTION 4
As You Read
Sample answer: Blockade: British blockade
hurt the French; Invasion of Spain: Guerrillas
weakened the French; Invasion of Russia:
French defeated.

Summary
1. Napoleon invaded Russia, reached
Moscow, but lost thousands of his
soldiers. They either deserted or died from
cold, hunger, and attacks.
2. Napoleon's last attempt was called the
Hundred Days, which ended in his final
battle at Waterloo.

Graphic Organizer
Possible responses:
1. It weakened economies of France and
other lands under Napoleon's control more
than it damaged Britain.
2. Loss of many soldiers weakened French
Empire; enflamed nationalistic feelings

encouraged conquered peoples to turn against French.
3. Desperate French soldiers deserted in search of food because of Russian scorched-earth policy.
4. Unable to advance further, French soldiers retreated; all but 10,000 died of exhaustion, hunger, and the cold.
5. Coalition defeated inexperienced French army; Napoleon's empire crumbled.
6. European armies defeated French forces and ended Napoleon's last bid for power.

SECTION 5
As You Read
Sample answer: Problems: 1. Contain France; 2. Establish a government for France. Solutions: 1. Surround France with stronger countries; 2. Restore the French monarchy.

Summary
1. Metternich's goals were to make sure that the French would not attack another country again, to create a balance of power, and to return monarchs to the thrones that they had been forced to leave.
2. Many European rulers did not encourage ideas of independence or equal rights. Yet many ordinary people wanted equality and rights. Revolts occurred in the Americas. National feelings grew.

Graphic Organizer
Possible responses:
Members and Representatives: Five European "great powers"—Austria, Prussia, and Russia represented by their rulers and Britain and France by their foreign ministers
Goals: Establish lasting peace and stability in Europe; prevent future French aggression; restore balance of power; restore royal families to thrones
Actions Taken: Formed Kingdom of the Netherlands; created German Confederation; recognized independence of Switzerland; added Genoa to Kingdom of Sardinia; required France to return territories conquered by Napoleon but left France a major power; affirmed principle of legitimacy

Legacy: Short-term: Conservatives regained control of governments; triggered revolts in colonies Long-term: Created an age of peace in Europe; diminished power of France and increased power of Britain and Prussia; sparked growth of nationalism

Nationalist Revolutions Sweep the West

SECTION 1
As You Read
Sample answer: Haiti: Enslaved Africans on the western third of the island of Hispaniola in the Caribbean Sea; from 1791 to 1804; to gain freedom from slavery. Spanish South America: Creoles in Spanish South America (led by Simón Bolívar and José de San Martin); from 1810 to 1824; to gain independence from the illegitimate Spanish crown. Mexico: Indians and mestizos in Mexico initially, but creoles later; from 1810 to 1821; better lives for the poor, initially, but later creoles fought to maintain their privileges. Brazil: creoles in Brazil led by Dom Pedro, son of Portugal's King John; 1822; to stop Brazil from returning to its former state as a colony of Portugal.

Summary
1. Peninsulares, creoles
2. The slaves revolted and then declared their independence.
3. Simón Bolívar led the fight in Venezuela; José de San Martín led the fight in Chile and Argentina.
4. Mexicans fought for independence, while Brazilians asked for independence and achieved it through a bloodless revolt.

Graphic Organizer
Possible responses:
1. Whites used brutal methods to terrorize and dehumanize them, trying to keep them powerless; slaves outnumbered their masters.
2. Toussaint L'Ouverture became the leader of the revolution, but the French

imprisoned him. Then General Dessalines took over the rebellion.

3. Motivated by Enlightenment ideals, creoles finally revolted against Spanish colonial rule when Napoleon made his brother, who was not Spanish, king of Spain.

4. Bolívar used surprise tactics to defeat the Spanish in Bogotá. San Martín, with the help of Bernardo O'Higgins, drove the Spanish out of Chile. The two leaders then met in Ecuador and San Martín left his army for Bolívar to command; this unified revolutionary force, under Bolívar, won independence for Peru.

5. With the *cry of Dolores,* Padre Miguel Hidalgo called upon peasants to rebel against Spanish rule.

6. Indians and mestizos began the revolution; later, creoles, fearing the loss of privileges under a new liberal regime in Spain, supported independence.

SECTION 2
As You Read
Sample answer: 1821: Greece rebels against Ottomans; 1830: Belgians rebel against Dutch, Poles rebel against Russia, French depose Charles X; 1848: Hungarians demand self-government and Czechs demand Bohemian independence from Austria; liberal revolt in German states; French demand democratic government.

Summary
1. Conservatives supported the kings; liberals wanted to give more power to elected legislatures; radicals wanted to end rule by kings and give full voting rights to all.
2. Greek, Belgians, Italians, Poles, Hungarians, and Czechs
3. He built roads, helped industry, and improved the economy.
4. Czar Alexander III freed the serfs.

Graphic Organizer
Possible responses:
1. fueled nationalist movements and revolutions throughout Europe

2. A joint British, French, and Russian fleet defeated the Ottomans, and Greece gained its independence.

3. forced resignation of Metternich, triggered liberal uprisings throughout German states, but revolutionaries' failure to unite led to return of conservatism

4. led to riots that forced him to flee to Britain and led to replacement by Louis-Philippe, a supporter of liberal reforms

5. Republican government is set up, but factions turn to violence, resulting in bloody battles.

6. Under this strong ruler, prosperity, peace, and stability were restored.

7. Russia was defeated by combined forces of France, Great Britain, Sardinia, and the Ottomans; after the war, Alexander II began to modernize Russia.

8. Serfs were legally free but remained tied to the land through debts.

SECTION 3
As You Read
Sample answer: Italy: 1848 Cavour appointed prime minister; 1858 French help drive out Austria; 1860 Garibaldi gives up power to King Victor Emmanuel. Germany: 1862 Bismarck appointed prime minister; 1866 Seven Weeks' War; 1870 Franco-Prussian War.

Summary
1. *Possible answer:* common nationality or ethnic ancestry and shared language, culture, history, and religion.
2. The Austrian Empire, Russia, and the Ottoman Empire were torn apart by nationalism.
3. Camillo di Cavour unified northern Italy; Giuseppe Garibaldi unified southern Italy.
4. These events changed the balance of power in Europe.

Graphic Organizer
Possible responses:
1. Nationalist disputes led to the division of the empire into two states, Austria and Hungary. After World War I, the empire divided into separate nation-states.

2. Nationalist feeling of non-Russian peoples, fueled by the policy of Russification, weakened the empire, which fell as a result of war and revolution.

3. Conservative Turks, angered by the Ottoman policy of granting equal citizenship to nationalist groups, caused tensions that weakened and eventually broke up the empire.

4. as prime minister of Sardinian king, worked to expand Sardinian empire; through war, alliances, and help of nationalist rebels, succeeded; in the process, unified Italy

5. captured Sicily and united the southern areas of Italy he conquered with kingdom of Piedmont-Sardinia

6. pulled together northern and southern regions of Italy and took over the Papal states unifying Italy

7. This policy of tough politics allowed Bismarck to expand Prussia and achieve dominance over Germany.

8. Victory over Austria gave Prussia control over northern Germany.

9. Victory over France motivated southern Germany to accept Prussian leadership.

SECTION 4
As You Read
Sample answer: I. A. The ideas of Romanticism, B. Romanticism in literature, C. The Gothic novel, D. Composers emphasize emotion; II. A. Photographers capture reality, B. Writers study society; III. A. Life in the moment

Summary
1. Romantic thinkers and artists valued feeling over reason and nature over society.

2. Writers used realism to show what life was truly like and to protest unfair social conditions.

3. Impressionists focused on a moment in time or an impression of a subject.

Graphic Organizer
Possible responses:
1. emphasized emotions over reason, untamed nature over natural laws and order; idealized past

2. Romantic writers glorified heroes and heroic actions, passionate love, revolutionary spirit, nature, and the supernatural.

3. Romantic painters focused on the beauty of nature, love, religion, and nationalism.

4. Romantic themes helped to popularize music and celebrate heroism and nationalism.

5. industrialization, interest in scientific method, invention of camera

6. The camera made possible startlingly real and objective images.

7. struggle for wealth and power, grim lives of working class

8. They hoped to bring about social reform and improve working and living conditions.

The Industrial Revolution

SECTION 1
As You Read
Sample answer: 1701: seed drill; 1733: flying shuttle; 1764: spinning jenny; 1765: steam engine; 1769: water frame; 1779: spinning mule; 1787: power loom; 1793: cotton gin; 1825: railroad opens.

Summary
1. Britain had the resources for industrialization, including coal, water, iron ore, rivers, harbors, and banks. Britain also had all the factors for production.

2. *Possible answer:* The textile industry had to move into factories because the new machines were so large.

3. The steam engine helped power machines in factories and led to breakthroughs in transportation on land and water.

Graphic Organizer
Possible responses:

1. Increased food supplies led to an increase in population that boosted demand for manufactured goods and provided labor for factories.
2. Britain had the natural resources needed for industrialization: water power, coal, iron ore, rivers, and harbors.
3. enabled Britain to devote its energies and resources to economic expansion, industrialization, and overseas trade; created a climate for progress
4. Britain had all the resources needed to produce goods and services, including land, labor, and capital.
5. improved the quality and speed of cotton cloth production; boosted profits; spurred other industrial improvements
6. provided organization and management skills and took financial risks of developing new businesses
7. allowed industry to move out of the home and into a central location
8. provided an inexpensive way to transport raw materials and manufactured products; created new jobs

SECTION 2
As You Read

Sample answer: I. A. Population growth, B. Living and working conditions deteriorate. II. A. Middle class prospers, B. Working class protests. III. A. Improved standard of living, B. Increased hope for improvement. IV. A. Great wealth for merchants, B. Pollution, C. Child labor.

Summary

1. *Possible answer:* People moved from the country to the city and found jobs where they worked 14 hours a day, 6 days a week.
2. *Possible answer:* Three positive effects were the creation of wealth, jobs, and better living conditions. Three negative effects were harsh working conditions; crowded, dirty conditions in cities; short life spans in cities.

3. *Possible answer:* Manchester experienced rapid growth in population and jobs. The city became crowded and polluted. Some people grew very rich.

Graphic Organizer
Possible responses:

1. Because no plans, sanitary codes, or building regulations controlled the rampant growth of English cities, the poor lacked adequate housing and many were forced to live in dark, filthy, overcrowded slums under very unhealthy and unsafe conditions.
2. Because factory owners wanted to keep their machines running for as many hours a day as possible, workers were forced to work long hours for starvation wages, often under dangerous and unhealthy conditions; later, working conditions and the standard of living improved.
3. They gained wealth and status in society and joined a growing middle class of skilled workers, professionals, business people, and well-to-do farmers.
4. Children as young as six began to work in factories with their families for long hours under brutal conditions; child labor laws later brought some reforms.
5. They enjoyed a comfortable standard of living.
6. Because some factory owners, merchants, and investment bankers grew wealthier, they lost some status, respect, and power but continued to look down on those who gained wealth in business.
7. The environment was polluted and natural resources were depleted.
8. Educational opportunities expanded in response to a need for skilled and professional workers.

SECTION 3
As You Read

Sample answer: U.S.: political unity, large distances; Both: began in textiles, railroads important, resources important; Europe: slowed by geography and social structure.

Summary

1. The United States had the resources needed for industrialization. Industrialization first occurred in the production of textiles. The first factories were built in the Northeast.
2. After England, Belgium was the first nation to industrialize. The western parts of Germany soon followed. France began to industrialize after 1830.
3. European nations needed raw materials for their factories and markets for their goods. European nations hoped to get both of these things from colonies.

Graphic Organizer

Possible responses:

1. water power, harbors, iron ore, coal, vast labor force, political stability, favorable financial system
2. technological boom, expansion of railroads, formation of corporations, available capital
3. delayed industrialization because war halted communications and trade, drained resources, and caused inflation and political instability
4. Industrialization was regional rather than nationwide; some countries did not industrialize because of geographic or social obstacles.
5. widened existing inequalities between industrialized and nonindustrialized countries and paved the way for imperialism
6. created opportunities for achieving wealth, a comfortable standard of living, education, a higher life expectancy, and democratic and social reforms

SECTION 4

As You Read

Sample answer: Capitalism: 1. Laws of competition, self-interest, supply and demand; 2. Middle and working classes; 3. Private property and production ownership; 4. government doesn't interfere. Socialism: 1. community property and production ownership; 2. community protects workers; 3. classless society.

Summary

1. Capitalism is an economic system in which people invest their money to make a profit.
2. In capitalism, people invest their money to make a profit to keep for themselves. Socialism aims to have people share equally in the wealth they create.
3. Workers tried to improve their lives by forming unions to fight for better working conditions. When employers resisted these efforts, workers sometimes went on strike. Britain passed reform laws that limited how much women and children could work. Groups in the United States pushed for similar laws.
4. Two major movements for change were the movement for the abolition of slavery and the struggle for women's rights.

Graphic Organizer

Possible responses:

1. Economic liberty guaranteed economic progress; government need not interfere in the economy.
2. Population tended to increase more rapidly than food supply; without wars and epidemics to kill off extra population, most people would always be poor.
3. The permanent underclass would always be poor because wages would be forced down as population increased and more workers became available.
4. Mill wanted government to do away with great differences in wealth; he favored a more equal division of profits, a cooperative system of agriculture, and women's rights such as the right to vote.
5. He improved working and living conditions for employees in his mills by renting them low-rent housing that he built, prohibiting children under ten from working in his mills, and providing free schooling. He also founded a cooperative utopian community.
6. They advocated socialism, under which the factors of production would be owned

by the public and operated for the benefit of all, as a replacement for free-market capitalism.

7. They predicted the destruction of the capitalist system and the creation of a classless communist state in which the means of production would be owned by the people.

8. He led the fight in Parliament for the end of the slave trade and slavery in the British Empire.

9. She ran a settlement house to provide social services to residents of a poor neighborhood.

10. He called for free public schooling for all children.

The Age of Democracy and Progress

SECTION 1
As You Read
Sample answer: Britain gradually extends suffrage to most adult males; important because government became more representative. Women in many counties demand the right to vote; greatest expansion of democracy because half the population of the planet is female. Dreyfus Affair in France; important because related to anti-Semitism and Zionism.

Summary
1. Britain became more democratic as more people got the right to vote and other rights.
2. Women in both countries did not get the right to vote until after World War I.
3. It was found in France and other European countries in Eastern Europe, such as Russia.

Graphic Organizer
Possible responses:
1. Fearing political protests might turn into revolution, they passed political reforms that eased the property requirement for voting so that well-off men in the middle class could vote.

2. It extended the vote to upper middleclass men by easing property requirements and gave industrial cities more representation in Parliament. Passage of the bill also encouraged other reformers to push for more rights.

3. Democratic reforms enacted in the 1800s had shifted power from the monarchy to the legislature, Parliament.

4. universal male suffrage, annual Parliamentary elections, the secret ballot, end to property requirements for serving in Parliament, pay for members of Parliament

5. to correct the ills of industrialization and urbanization, improve conditions for workers and the poor, acquire the rights for women that men had

6. to draw attention to the cause of women's suffrage; to win suffrage for women

SECTION 2
As You Read
Sample answer: Canda: Dominion 1867; Australia and New Zealand: Self-governing 1850s, dominions early 1900s; Ireland: Southern home rule 1921, Irish Free State becomes independent 1949.

Summary
1. French speakers still lived in the colony from the time when Canada was controlled from France. England eventually took this land over.

2. The Maoris of New Zealand kept their rights to the land. The Aborigines of Australia had almost no rights.

3. English Protestants lived in the north, and Irish Catholics lived in the south. The British feared the Catholic majority would be unfair to the Protestant minority.

Graphic Organizer
Possible responses:
1. Causes: religious and cultural differences between mostly Roman Catholic French and mainly English-speaking Protestants in Canada; pressure from both groups for a greater voice in governing their own affairs

Effects: Each province got its own elected assembly, temporarily easing tensions until later rebellions led to reunification.

2. Causes: Many Canadians felt Canada needed a central government to protect against territorial expansion by the United States.
Effects: established self-government for Canada in domestic affairs; led to westward expansion and economic development

3. Causes: Conflicts between Maoris and European settlers over land led the settlers to plead for annexation.
Effects: Maori acceptance of British rule in return for permanent title to their lands.

4. Causes: British determination to keep control over Ireland
Effects: setback for Irish nationalism; representation for Ireland in Parliament; passage of Catholic Emancipation Act, which restored many rights to Catholics

5. Causes: pressure from English landowners
Effects: Many Irish lost their land and fell hopelessly in debt, while large landowners profited from higher food prices.

6. Causes: Irish frustration over delay in independence plans
Effects: continued bitterness, violence, and unrest resulting in division of Ireland in 1921

SECTION 3
As You Read
Sample answer: 1803: Louisiana Purchase; 1819: Florida Cession; 1845: Texas Annexation; 1846: British treaty; 1848: Mexican Cession; 1853: Gadsden Purchase; 1869: transcontinental railroad

Summary
1. The movement westward caused suffering for thousands of Native Americans who were forced to move.
2. The Emancipation Proclamation was issued. A brief period of equal rights for African Americans followed.
3. Immigration helped cause the rise in industrial growth.

Graphic Organizer
Possible responses:
1. almost doubled the size of the U.S. and extended western boundary to the Rocky Mountains
2. acquired Florida from Spain and part of the Oregon Territory by treaty with Britain
3. California and much of the Southwest
4. led to eviction of Native Americans from their tribal lands, since government leaders used manifest destiny as a way to justify any action that helped white settlers occupy new land
5. country's westward expansion and expansion of slavery, economic differences, issue of states' rights to leave the union
6. election of Abraham Lincoln, secession of Southern states, Confederate forces' firing on Fort Sumter
7. to help achieve his goal of preserving the Union; to show European nations that the war was being fought against slavery
8. expansion of industry, trade, railroads

SECTION 4
As You Read
Sample answer: Edison's electric light; Ford's assembly line; Pasteur's germ theory; Darwin's theory of evolution

Summary
1. *Possible answers:* The light bulb, phonograph, radio, and telephone were three key inventions.
2. Pasteur's discovery of bacteria enabled scientists to develop methods to kill disease-causing germs.
3. Darwin developed the theory of evolution, Mendel began the science of genetics, and the Curies discovered radioactivity.
4. Freud revealed that the subconscious mind shaped behavior.
5. Silent movies, sporting events, and music halls became popular.

Graphic Organizer
Possible responses:
1. inventions including electric light bulb, phonograph, motion pictures, and the idea

of a laboratory for industrial research and development
2. harnessed electricity to transmit sounds by telephone
3. created first radio
4. introduced assembly line and used standardized, interchangeable parts to make cars that were affordable to many people
5. designed first powered flying machine
6. developed process of pasteurization, using heat to kill bacteria
7. advanced theory of evolution that new species develop, or evolve, through natural selection
8. began science of genetics by discovering that there is a pattern to the way certain traits are inherited
9. discovered radium and polonium, two radioactive elements, and did important work on radioactivity
10. broke new ground in psychology by experimenting and concluding that human actions can be changed through training

The Age of Imperialism

SECTION 1
As You Read
Sample answer: I. A. Diverse peoples, B. Trading networks. II. A. Racism, B. Social Darwinism, C. Technological superiority, D. Medical advances.

Summary
1. There are four reasons for imperialism: the desire for raw materials and new markets, nationalism, racism, and the missionary desire to convert people.
2. The Berlin Conference was held to keep European nations from fighting over African lands.
3. The Boers were Dutch farmers in South Africa who fought against the Zulus and the British for control over South Africa.

Graphic Organizer
Possible responses:
1. economic competition for markets and raw materials, national pride, racism, and

missionaries' desire to Christianize and "civilize" non-European peoples
2. superior weapons; railroads, cables, and steamships; quinine to protect from malaria
3. Africans' great diversity of languages and cultures, ethnic rivalries, lower level of technology including weapons
4. agreement among 14 European nations about how to divide Africa among European countries; arbitrary distribution of African ethnic and linguistic groups among European nations; transformation of the way of life of Africans
5. Zulus, Boers (Dutch), and British
6. creation of self-governing Union of South Africa controlled by British

SECTION 2
As You Read
Sample answer: Forms and methods: Colony, protectorate, sphere of influence, economic imperialism, direct control, indirect control; Resistance: Movements in all but Ethiopia failed; Impact: Societies and cultures devastated, traditional boundaries ignored.

Summary
1. The four forms of control were colony, protectorate, sphere of influence, and economic imperialism. The two management methods were direct and indirect control.
2. The Algerians resisted the French. East Africans resisted the Germans. Ethiopians successfully resisted the Italians.
3. *Possible answer:* Three benefits were ends to ethnic conflict, improvements in transportation, and improvements in communication. Three problems were the breakdown of traditional society, forced movement, and the loss of local political control.

Graphic Organizer
Possible responses:
1. indirectly by allowing existing political rulers to govern under British authority and local officials to manage daily affairs

2. direct control through policies of paternalism and assimilation
3. Algeria used active resistance, whereas East Africans used a spiritual defense that included the belief that magic water sprinkled on their bodies would ward off European bullets.
4. Emperor Menelik II took advantage of rivalries among Italians, French, and British to build an arsenal. He later declared war and defeated the Italians at the Battle of Adowa.
5. Colonialism reduced local warfare; in some colonies it improved education, sanitation, transportation, and communication for the Africans. In addition, African products came to be valued on the international market.
6. death from European diseases to which Africans had previously not been exposed and from active resistance to European rule, loss of property, famine, breakdown in traditional way of life, artificial political divisions that would lead to ethnic and civil wars

SECTION 3
As You Read
Sample answer: Details: Ottoman Empire tries to reform but fails; Egyptian leaders cannot complete modernization; Persia falls to economic imperialism.

Summary
1. Greece and Serbia won self-rule. Europeans scrambled for the rest.
2. To gain control of the Black Sea and to extend its empire
3. Both tried to modernize, but Britain took control of Egypt and Britain and Russia took control of Persia.

Graphic Organizer
Possible responses:
1. a succession of weak rulers, division into factions, corruption, economic and technological decline
2. inspired Greeks, Serbs, and other groups in Ottoman Empire to fight for self-rule

3. World powers formed alliances or waged war to gain control of the Ottoman Empire because of its strategic geographic location.
4. When Egypt ran into problems paying for the construction, Britain insisted on overseeing financial control of the canal and, in 1882, occupied the country.
5. Lacking capital to develop its resources, Persia granted concessions to European businesses; rebellion followed, and eventually Britain and Russia divided Persia into spheres of influence.

SECTION 4
As You Read
Sample answer: Effects: 1. East India Company expanded its colonial territory; 2. Created resentment and nationalistic feelings among Indians; 3. Built support for nationalist groups.

Summary
1. *Possible answer:* British rule brought resentment, poverty, and suffering for many Indians. British rule also damaged Indian culture.
2. The Sepoy Mutiny was an uprising of Indian soldiers in the service of the British who were offended by British attitudes, especially toward their religion.
3. Both the Indian National Congress and the Muslim League called for self-government for India.

Graphic Organizer
Possible responses:
1. Led by Robert Clive, company troops defeated Indian forces at the Battle of Plassey after Mughal rule had become weak.
2. Railroads transported raw products from the interior to the ports and manufactured goods from the coast into the interior; India became more profitable for Britain; India developed a modern economy and was geographically unified.
3. British restricted Indian-owned industries such as cotton textiles and reduced food production in favor of cash crops.

4. British government assumed direct control of India; racism and mutual distrust were intensified.
5. calls by reformers for India to modernize, nationalist feelings, resentment over British discriminatory policies
6. Acts of terrorism forced British to divide province in a different way to avoid open rebellion.

SECTION 5
As You Read
Sample answer: Dutch: Indonesia; British: Malay Peninsula; French: Indochina; U.S.: Philippines, Hawaii.

Summary
1. Colonialism mixed cultures and religions and often resulted in conflict.
2. Siam modernized and played the French and British against one another to remain free.
3. After the United States won possession of the Philippines, Filipinos fought for their freedom. After the United States defeated them, it promised the Filipinos self-rule later. Meanwhile, U.S. businesses took advantage of the Filipino workers.

Graphic Organizer
Possible responses:
1. Lands: Malacca, Java, Sumatra, part of Borneo, Celebes, the Moluccas, Bali, finally all Indonesia
   Products: oil, tin, rubber
   Impact of colonization: creation of rigid social class
2. Lands: Malay Peninsula, Burma
   Immigration: encouraged Chinese to immigrate to Malaysia
   Impact of colonization: racial conflict between Malay minority and Chinese immigrant majority
3. Lands: Vietnam, Laos, Cambodia
   Management: direct colonial management
   Impact of colonization: decline of local industries, less food for peasants
4. Lands: Guam, Philippine Islands, Puerto Rico, Hawaii

Management: some preparation for colonial self-rule
Impact of colonization: economic exploitation, modernization of transportation, health, and education systems

Transformations Around the Globe
SECTION 1
As You Read
Sample answer: Internal: Growing population, corrupt officials opposed to reform, inability to handle external problems. External: Influence of foreign powers, extraterritorial rights for foreigners, growing opium trade.

Summary
1. Britain took possession of Hong Kong. Later, other countries won extraterritorial rights and the right to trade in five Chinese ports.
2. The Taiping Rebellion was a revolt against the Qing Dynasty, which had many internal problems. The revolt was led by Hong Xiuquan. The rebellion was put down after 14 years of fighting. Much farmland was destroyed.
3. European powers and Japan gained a sphere of influence. Later, the United States urged support for an Open Door Policy. This policy would allow more nations to have access to markets in China.
4. The Boxer Rebellion was a war fought by Chinese peasants and workers against the presence of foreigners in China. A multinational army put down the rebellion.

Graphic Organizer
Possible responses:
1. Causes: Britain's refusal to stop opium trade
   Effects: Chinese defeat and humiliation; cession of Hong Kong to Britain; continuation of opium trade; extraterritorial rights for foreign citizens; Chinese resentment against foreigners

2. Causes: hunger and starvation caused by inability to feed enormous population; increasing opium addiction; poverty
Effects: restoration of Qing to power, at least 20 million people died

3. Causes: need to modernize education, diplomatic service, and military; support of Dowager Empress
Effects: ability to produce its own warships and ammunition

4. Causes: China's weak military, economic and political problems; division of China into Western spheres of influence; U.S fears that China would be divided into formal colonies and American traders would be shut out
Effects: protection of American trading rights in China; keeping China free from colonization; continued economic imperialism in China

5. Causes: Chinese people's long-standing frustration with poor conditions and government failure to reform; anger over special privileges granted to foreigners; resentment of Chinese Christians; failure of Guangxu's reform efforts
Effects: failure to effect reforms; emergence of sense of nationalism; Qing court's beginning steps toward reform

SECTION 2
As You Read
Sample answer: Modernization: Military, government, and education. Imperialism: Defeat of China, Russia, Korean takeover.

Summary
1. Mutsuhito sent officials to other countries to learn their ways. He used other governments and militaries as a model for Japan. He reformed the economy to make it more modern.
2. Japan fought wars against China and Russia and took territory from each nation. Then Japan attacked and annexed Korea.

Graphic Organizer
Possible responses:
1. to shock and frighten the Japanese into accepting trade with the United States

2. gained right to trade at two ports in Japan
3. adapted aspects of foreign cultures they admired, such as the American education system and Germany's centralized government and military discipline; followed the Western path to industrialization and developed modern industries
4. for trade and as a military outpost to protect their own security
5. Rebellion broke out against Korea's king, who asked China for military help. Chinese troops marched into Korea. Japan protested violation of agreement and sent its troops to fight the Chinese.
6. destruction of Chinese navy, beginning of Japanese colonial empire, change to world's balance of power, emergence of Russia and Japan as major powers— and enemies—in East Asia
7. Russian refusal to stay out of Korea led to a Japanese surprise attack on the Russian navy anchored off the coast of Manchuria.
8. destruction of Russian navy; territorial gains for Japan, withdrawal of Russia from Manchuria and Korea
9. harshly; established very repressive government that denied rights to Koreans; inspired Korean nationalist movement

SECTION 3
As You Read
Sample answer: 1823: Monroe Doctrine; 1898: Spanish-American War; 1903: Panamanian rebellion; 1914: Panama Canal opened.

Summary
1. Most people were poor laborers. Wealthy landowners took advantage of poor farmers. Only people who owned property were allowed to vote. There was political unrest caused by military leaders who competed for power.
2. Latin American nations had to pay more for imports than they made on their exports. They went into debt to foreign banks. These foreign interests had a great

deal of control over Latin American affairs.

3. The United States helped the people of Panama revolt against Colombia, which originally had the land. Then the United States took control of a ten-mile-wide zone in Panama.

Graphic Organizer

Possible responses:

1. Landowners forced workers into debt by paying low wages with vouchers that could be used only at supply stores that were run by the landowners. Prices there were high, so workers were always in debt.

2. unevenly, with land ownership restricted to a wealthy few

3. People had little or no experience with democracy and were used to political power being restricted to a few; rule by caudillos, or dictators, often resulted.

4. increased Latin American exports but kept Latin America dependent on importing manufactured goods

5. Foreign lenders took over Latin American industries in payment for unpaid loans with high interest rates.

6. Latin American nations focused only on their exports and saw no reason to industrialize as they imported manufactured goods from Europe and North America.

1. to protect the independence of Latin American nations and the security of the United States

2. The U.S. gained the rest of Spain's colonial empire; the Monroe Doctrine prevented powerful European nations from building empires in the Americas.

3. by building the Panama Canal, setting up a military government in Cuba, investing in Central and South American countries, and using troops to intervene in Latin American countries

SECTION 4

As You Read

Sample answer: Juárez: Land education reform; Madero: Revolution; Carranza: Revised constitution; Obregón: Land reform.

Summary

1. Texas declared independence from Mexico. The United States annexed Texas, and Mexico and the United States went to war. The United States won the war, and Mexico lost huge amounts of land to the United States.

2. Conservatives made a secret plan with Napoleon III of France to take Mexico back from the reformers led by Juárez.

3. Díaz brought order to the country, ended raids by gangs of bandits, and helped create some economic growth. However, he also limited political freedom.

4. Goals included better lives for the poor, especially land for the poor.

Graphic Organizer

Possible responses:

1. instrumental in fight for independence from Spain, led Mexican forces against Texans, ruled as president four times between 1833 and 1855; left a legacy of military defeats, loss of territory to U.S.

2. began reforms, fought against French rule; left a legacy of peace, progress, and reform

3. fought against the French, restored order, stabilized currency, encouraged foreign investments; left a legacy of harsh rule, rising food prices, and exploitation of peasants

4. began Mexican Revolution with his push for democratic government and call for armed revolt against Díaz

5. assembled an army in the north and won important victories against Díaz's army and later Huerta's forces

6. raised a powerful revolutionary army and helped defeat Díaz and overthrow Huerta

7. overthrew Huerta, seized control of the government, and murdered Zapata, thus ending civil war in Mexico

The Great War

SECTION 1

As You Read

Sample answer: Events: rise of European nationalism, imperialism, arms race, Bismarck's unification of German, formation of Triple Alliance, Wilhelm II's shipbuilding program, formation of Triple Entente, Austria-Hungary's annexation of Bosnia and Herzegovina, assassination of Archduke Franz Ferdinand.

Summary

1. Nationalism, imperialism, and militarism all helped lead to war.
2. One group was Britain, France, and Russia; the other was Germany, Austria-Hungary, and Italy.
3. Serbia had troubles with Austria over control of Bosnia and Herzegovina. A Serbian killed the heir to the throne of Austria-Hungary. As a result, Austria-Hungary declared war on Serbia. Soon most of Europe was at war

Graphic Organizer

Possible responses:

1. a. deep devotion to one's nation
   b. caused intense competition by the turn of the 20th century among Europe's Great Powers (Germany, Austria-Hungary, Great Britain, Russia, Italy, and France) for industrial dominance and power
2. a. quest for colonies
   b. intensified European nations' sense of rivalry and mistrust toward one another as they competed for colonies in Asia and Africa
3. a. policy of glorifying military power and keeping an army prepared for war and able to mobilize troops quickly in case of a war
   b. led to an arms race and formation of large standing armies and, eventually, to military alliances
4. a. agreement crafted by Bismarck, who saw France as a threat to peace, that

made Germany, Austria-Hungary, and Italy military allies
   b. created an unstable and fragile alliance that tried to isolate France
5. a. alliance among Britain, France, and Russia, in which Britain pledged not to fight France and Russia
   b. established two rival camps in Europe—Triple Alliance and Triple Entente—that created the possibility that any dispute between two rival powers could draw the entire continent into war
6. a. A Serbian nationalist murders Archduke Franz Ferdinand, heir to the Austro-Hungarian throne, and his wife.
   b. provided Austria-Hungary with an excuse to launch war on Serbia, leading to a confrontation between Austria and Russia

SECTION 2

As You Read

Sample answer: I. A. Germany declares war on Russia and France, B. Great Britain declares war on Germany, C. Central Powers and Allies form. II. A. Germany pursues Schlieffen Plan, B. Allies win at Marne. III. Eastern Front, A. Germany and Austria push Russia back, B. Russia holds off Germany.

Summary

1. The Allies were France, Britain, and Russia (later joined by Italy). The Central Powers were Bulgaria, the Ottoman Empire, Germany, and Austria-Hungary.
2. The war on the Western Front was bloody and brutal. Trench warfare began. Outside the trenches, soldiers faced powerful weapons, such as machine guns, poison gas, and tanks.
3. Possible response: Russia's undeveloped industrial economy was a major weakness. Russian troops had inadequate supplies. Russia's strength was its huge population. Millions of Russians could go to war.

Graphic Organizer

Possible responses:
1. Germany declares war on Russia and on France.
2. Britain declares war on Germany.
3. The Allies' victory destroys Germany's hopes for the Schlieffen Plan, which called for a quick victory in the west, and suggests that Germany may have to fight a long war on two fronts.
4. The new technology turns the Western Front into a horrible and horrifying "terrain of death" in which huge numbers of soldiers die.
5. Germany counterattacks, forces Russian forces to retreat, and regains East Prussia. Austrian forces drive the Russians out of Austria-Hungary.
6. Because Russia is not industrialized, its war effort is short of supplies and near collapse.

SECTION 3
As You Read
Sample answer: Effects: Millions dead, Land destroyed, Economies shattered, Mass disillusionment.

Summary
1. Arab nations, Southwest Asian countries, China, areas in the Pacific, Mexico, and the United States were all involved or affected the war.
2. Possible response: The war caused hardship through rationing, limited people's freedom to disagree, and changed people's attitudes about women's job skills.
3. Exhaustion and supply shortages weakened German soldiers. Kaiser Wilhelm II of Germany was forced to step down. In Austria-Hungary, the emperor was overthrown.
4. Possible responses: Political cost—8.5 million dead soldiers; economic cost—$338 billion in damage; emotional cost—a new sense of hopelessness.

Graphic Organizer

Possible responses:
1. The Allies believed that if they could secure the Dardanelles, the narrow sea strait that was the gateway to the Ottoman capital of Constantinople, they would be able to take Constantinople, defeat the Turks, and establish a supply line to Russia.
2. because of public outrage over Germany's unrestricted submarine warfare and the Zimmermann note, traditional bonds between Americans and English, reports of German war atrocities, and most importantly, strong economic ties with Allies
3. Czar Nicholas abdicated when he was faced with civil unrest due in part to wartime shortages, the refusal of the army to continue fighting, and the prospect of revolution.
4. it ended the war between Russia and Germany
5. The German war effort had exhausted both men and supplies; more than two million American troops took part in this battle; Allied forces began to advance steadily toward Germany and the Central Powers began to crumble.
6. surrender of Bulgarians and Ottoman Turks; revolution in Austria-Hungary; mutiny in Germany and forced resignation of Kaiser

SECTION 4
As You Read
Sample answer: Germany: Bitterness and hatred at costs exacted; Africans and Asians: Anger at lack of independence; Italy and Japan: Disappointment at lack of territory gained.

Summary
1. *Possible response:* The treaty blamed Germany for the war and took away German territory in Europe and its former colonies. The treaty also forced Germany to make payments to the Allies. Germans were bitter about the treaty's conditions.

2. Germany—resented taking all the blame; Japan and Italy—got few territorial gains; colonial peoples—did not receive independence

Graphic Organizer
Possible responses:
1. a just and lasting peace achieved by ending secret treaties; freedom of the seas, free trade, and reduced national armies and navies; adjustment of colonial claims with fairness toward colonial peoples; granting self-determination; and establishing a world peace organization
2. Britain and France were concerned with national security, stripping Germany of its war-making power, and punishing Germany.
3. Germany lost substantial territory, had severe restrictions placed on its military operations, and was forced to acknowledge "war guilt" and pay reparations to the Allies.
4. New countries were created from the Austrian-Hungarian Empire; Ottoman lands in southwest Asia were carved up into mandates rather than independent nations; Finland, Latvia, Estonia, and Lithuania became independent nations; Poland and Romania gained Russian territory.
5. The treaty created the League of Nations, an international association whose goal was to keep peace among nations.
6. Many Americans objected to the League of Nations, believing that the United States should stay out of European affairs.
7. Without U.S. support, the League of Nations was unable to take action on various complaints of nations around the world.
8. The war guilt clause left a legacy of hatred among the Germans; Africans and Asians were angry that their desire for independence was ignored; Japanese and Italians gained less land than they wanted.

Revolution and Nationalism

SECTION 1
As You Read
Sample answer: 1894: Nicholas II becomes czar; 1917: Czarist rule ends; 1918–1920: Civil war; 1922: Union of Soviet Socialist Republics formed

Summary
1. Reforms stopped. People who were non-Russians or who disagreed with the czar were mistreated.
2. The Bolsheviks were a revolutionary group led by Lenin.
3. Possible answer: A massacre, strikes, resistance to the war, inflation, starvation, weak leadership, and corruption all contributed to bringing out the revolution.
4. Kerensky was the leader of the provisional government. He lost support by trying to keep Russia in the war.
5. The civil war was fought between Lenin's forces—the Red Army— and Lenin's opponents.
6. Lenin rebuilt the economy and changed the government to form the Soviet Union.

Graphic Organizer
Possible responses:
1. Autocratic policies, harsh measures, and resistance to change inflamed the masses.
2. Grueling working conditions, miserably low wages, and child labor, as well as the workers' low standard of living, lack of political power, the enormous gap between the rich and poor, led to civil unrest and strife.
3. Russia's losses sparked unrest at home, revealed the czar's weaknesses, and led to revolt in the middle of the war.
4. provoked a wave of strikes and violence across the country and forced Czar Nicholas II to promise more freedom and create the Duma, Russia's first parliament
5. revealed weaknesses of czarist rule and military leadership; destroyed morale of

Russian soldiers, who mutinied, deserted, and ignored orders

6. forced the czar, Nicholas II, to abdicate his throne; allowed Duma to set up provisional government
7. toppled provisional government and gave power to Bolsheviks
8. caused millions of deaths from fighting and famine; showed that Bolsheviks were able both to seize power and to maintain it; crushed opposition to Bolshevik rule
9. centralized power and unified country
10. Marx's ideas formed the basis of the revolutionary government.
11. led the Bolshevik revolution and restored peace and order
12. helped negotiate Treaty of Brest-Litovsk and commanded the Red Army during civil war

SECTION 2

As You Read

Sample answer: 1. Police Terror: Great Purge, liquidation of kulaks; 2. Propaganda: Government-controlled media; 3. Indoctrination: Education and training; 4. Persecution: Elimination of leadership.

Summary

1. Police terror, control of schools, propaganda, censorship, or persecution
2. Stalin's enemies
3. Possible answer: Since Stalin used the country's resources to speed up industrialization, people lacked food, housing, and clothing for many years. Those who resisted Stalin's farming revolution were killed or imprisoned.
4. Women had equal rights and chances for new careers. People were more educated.

Graphic Organizer

Possible responses:

1. initiated Five-Year Plans to promote industrial growth; limited production of consumer goods
2. established collective farms; eliminated wealthy peasants
3. controlled media; censored all forms of creativity; replaced religious teachings

with Communist ideals; persecuted the Russian Orthodox Church

4. expanded and controlled education at all levels; opened educational opportunities to women
5. used secret police and violent tactics to crush opposition; launched Great Purge
6. used indoctrination and art to glorify the Communist state; created state-supported youth groups to train future leaders

SECTION 3

As You Read

Sample answer: Jiang: 1. Head of Kuomintang, 2. Helped defeat warlords, 3. Forced the Long March; Mao: 1. Won peasants to cause by giving land, 2. promised reform, 3. survived Long March.

Summary

1. China's Nationalists wanted to modernize China and to get rid of foreign control over their country.
2. Possible answer: Jiang Jieshi fought the Communists. Then he rose to power representing those who feared the Communists.
3. The Japanese invasion of China temporarily united Communist and non-Communist forces.

Graphic Organizer

Possible responses:

1. Causes: belief among many Chinese that China needed to modernize and nationalize; years of humiliation under Qing Dynasty, during which foreign countries controlled China's trade and economic resources
   Effects: creation of new Republic of China and increase in nationalism
2. Causes: Sun lacked the authority and military support to secure national unity. Effects: Yuan, betraying the democratic ideals of the revolution, ruled as a dictator and sparked local revolts; power fell to warlords and chaos reigned; roads and bridges fell into disrepair, crops were destroyed, and many starved to death.

3. Causes: outrage over settlements in the Treaty of Versailles that gave Japan territories and privileges in China that had belonged to Germany

Effects: revealed Chinese people's commitment to goal of strengthening China; led to young Chinese intellectuals' turning against Sun's beliefs in Western democracy in favor of Lenin's brand of Soviet communism; led to formation of Chinese Communist Party

4. Causes: fear among Kuomintang followers that Chinese Communists would create a Socialist economy

Effects: purge of most Communist Party members; formal recognition of Nationalist government by Britain and United States; civil war

5. Causes: need for Communists to escape certain death by Jiang's Nationalist forces

Effects: survival of Mao and other Communist leaders; attraction of new followers to Communist cause; continuation of civil war

6. Causes: imperialist policy of Japan; weakened state of China

Effects: death of thousands of Chinese; destruction of farmland; halt to civil war as Nationalists and Communists temporarily united to fight Japan; beginning of World War II in Asia

SECTION 4
As You Read
Sample answer: Styles of government: Democratic self-rule—India; Republic—Turkey; Dictatorship—Iran; Monarchy—Saudi Arabia.

Summary
1. Possible answer: British control of Indian life, unfulfilled promises of the British, the jailing of protesters, and the massacre at Amritsar.
2. Indians stopped buying British goods, attending British schools, paying British taxes, and voting in British-run elections. In defiance, they broke unfair laws and staged protests.

3. Turkey and Saudi Arabia were formed. Persia became Iran.

Graphic Organizer
Possible responses:
1. began the effort to end foreign rule and achieve goal of national independence
2. intensified interest in self-government and expectations for postwar political reforms from Britain
3. Western-educated Indians felt that the Acts violated individual rights. Violent protests further inflamed radical nationalists.
4. angered millions of Indians and caused loyal British subjects in India to become revolutionaries and nationalists
5. weakened British authority and economic power
6. Peaceful demonstrations such as the Salt March further weakened British authority and gained worldwide support for Gandhi's independence movement.
7. When Greek soldiers invaded Turkey, military commander Mustafa Kemal led Turkish nationalists in overthrowing the weak Ottoman sultan.
8. The British attempt to take over Persia led to a nationalist revolt during which Reza Shah Pavlavi, an army officer, seized power.
9. Ibn Saud unified Arabia and renamed the new kingdom Saudi

Years of Crisis
SECTION 1
As You Read
Sample answer: Science: Albert Einstein, Sigmund Freud; Literature: Friedrich Nietzsche, James Joyce; Arts: Pablo Picasso, Arnold Schoenberg; Technology: Charles Lindbergh, Guglielmo Marconi.

Summary
1. Einstein developed the theory of relativity; Freud said that much of human behavior was irrational.
2. Existentialism is the belief that each person must make his or her own meaning

out of a world that has no universal meaning.
3. Cubism and surrealism arose.
4. Young people experimented with new values; women had more opportunities.
5. Changes in travel—more cars; more airplane flights.
Changes in entertainment—popularity of radio and motion pictures.

Graphic Organizer
Possible responses:
1. shattered the belief that the world operated according to absolute laws of motion and gravity
2. Because this theory hypothesized that much of human behavior is irrational, it weakened faith in reason.
3. taught that life had no universal meaning, leaving people to find their own meaning in life
4. inspired by Freud's ideas, sought to link world of dreams with real life in art
5. Composers moved away from traditional styles. The jazz beat was uninhibited and energetic, fitting the freedom and spontaneity of the times.
6. Women abandoned restrictive clothing and styles and argued that they should be equal partners with men.
7. created new manufacturing jobs and new businesses to serve car owners, expanded recreational travel, led to the growth of suburbs and a commuter population
8. Improvements in aircraft made possible commercial passenger service and international air travel.
9. expanded audiences for news, plays, and sporting events; helped bring world in closer touch
10. Movie-making became a serious art form in Europe and a major industry in Hollywood, and movies became a popular escape from daily hardships.

SECTION 2
As You Read
Sample answer: Effects: failed businesses, closed banks, lost savings, foreclosed farms, rising unemployment.

Summary
1. *Possible response:* The German government was weak; the economy was unstable.
2. *Possible response:* Falling food prices, sluggish sales, decrease in consumer spending, the stock market crash.
3. Franklin D. Roosevelt began a plan called the New Deal. The government created jobs and helped businesses and farmers.

Graphic Organizer
Possible responses:
1. Many citizens of the new democracies had little experience with representative government. Some countries had many political parties, which made effective government difficult and led to the formation of coalition governments that often unraveled.
2. Germany lacked a strong democratic tradition; postwar Germany had multiple political parties; many Germans blamed the Weimar government, not their wartime leaders, for the country's military defeat and humiliation at Versailles.
3. The German government had printed money for war expenses and reparations, devaluing the mark to the point where people needed wheelbarrows full of money to buy food.
4. uneven distribution of wealth, overproduction by business and agriculture, lessened demand for consumer goods
5. Believing that prices would drop, investors tried to sell high-priced stocks that they had bought on margin, but no one wanted to buy.
6. Unemployment rates rose as industrial production, prices, and wages fell; businesses failed, individuals lost their

savings when banks closed, and farmers lost their land.

7. Some countries had war debts and were dependent on American loans and investments. Worried American bankers demanded repayment for their overseas loans, and American investors withdrew their money from Europe. American market for imported goods dropped sharply. Raising of tariffs led to decrease in world trade and market demand.

8. passed high protective tariffs, increased taxes, regulated the currency, and lowered interest rates to encourage industrial growth

9. Economic crisis in France led to political instability and leaders feared the growth of antidemocratic forces.

10. relied on existing tradition of cooperative community action and government-sponsored public works programs to keep people employed and producing; raised pensions for the elderly and benefits for those in need

SECTION 3
As You Read

Sample answer: Hitler: Rise: appointed chancellor, became dictator, revived economy; Goals: regain lost land and take over more, purge country of "non-German" people. Mussolini: Rise: appointed leader, became dictator, took over economy; Goals: return Italy to ancient greatness.

Summary

1. Mussolini promised to help the economy and to build the armed forces.

2. He believed that Germans were superior, that the Treaty of Versailles was unfair, and that Germany needed more living space.

3. Hitler arrested his opponents, gave jobs to millions but took away their rights to organize, burned books, forced children to join Nazi groups, and attacked Germany's Jews.

4. Democracy survived there because these countries had strong democratic traditions.

Graphic Organizer
Possible responses:

1. Causes: Italians were disappointed by terms at Versailles and distressed by social unrest, rising inflation, and high unemployment. Mussolini promised to rescue Italy by reviving its economy and rebuilding its armed forces. He founded the Fascist party and rapidly gained popularity as economic conditions continued to worsen.
Effects: Mussolini publicly criticized the government; Fascists promoted a campaign of terror and gained support of middle classes, industrial leaders, and aristocracy.

2. Causes: The king decided that Mussolini was the best hope for his dynasty to survive.
Effects: Mussolini abolished democracy, outlawed all political parties but his Fascist party, imposed censorship, had his opponents jailed, outlawed strikes, and made allies of industrialists and large landowners.

3. Causes: He was a successful organizer and speaker.
Effects: The Nazis became a growing political force.

4. Causes: Inspired by Mussolini's march on Rome, Hitler and the Nazis tried to overthrow the government and seize power in Munich.
Effects: In jail, he wrote *Mein Kampf*, which set forth his beliefs and goals for Germany.

5. Causes: When the Depression ended the nation's brief postwar recovery, the German economy collapsed, civil unrest broke out, and the people looked to Hitler for strong leadership. Conservative leaders, believing they could control Hitler, advised von Hindenburg to name Hitler chancellor.
Effects: Hitler acted quickly to strengthen his position; he won a parliamentary majority in elections he called and turned Germany into a totalitarian state.

6. Causes: Hitler wanted to control every aspect of German life and shape public opinion.
   Effects: crushed opposition, forced conformity to Nazi beliefs
7. Causes: Anti-Semitism was a key part of Nazi ideology; Nazis used Jews as the scapegoats for Germany's troubles.
   Effects: Violence against Jews increased. *Kristallnacht* signaled the real start of the process of eliminating Jews from German life.

SECTION 4
As You Read
Sample answer: 1922: Agrees to respect China's borders; 1928: Signs Kellogg-Briand Pact; 1930: Military gains control; 1931: Invades Manchuria; 1936: Allies itself with Germany; 1937: Invades China

Summary
1. Japan invaded Manchuria and China.
2. Germany invaded parts of Germany that the Treaty of Versailles had deemed off limits to Germans. Italy invaded Ethiopia.
3. Britain, France, Italy, and Germany agreed to allow Germany to take land in Czechoslovakia under the condition that Germany would respect the new borders of Czechoslovakia.

Graphic Organizer
Possible responses:
1. to solve its economic problems and protect Japanese business interests
2. Britain and France hoped to keep the peace in Europe.
3. They hoped to keep the United States out of another war.
4. strengthened Hitler's power in Germany; tilted the balance of power in Germany's favor; encouraged Hitler to speed up military and territorial expansion
5. The Chinese retreated and set up a new capital; Chinese guerrillas continued to fight in the occupied area.
6. The Czechs were not invited. British prime minister Neville Chamberlain believed he could preserve peace by

giving in to Hitler's demands. When Hitler's troops took over Czechoslovakia, it was clear that the agreement had failed to stop Hitler from occupying Czechoslovakia and then demanding Danzig, Poland.
7. While the Western democracies remained neutral, Hitler and Mussolini sent troops, tanks, and airplanes to Franco.
8. Stalin wanted to avoid war with Germany.

World War II
SECTION 1
As You Read
Sample answer: Blitzkrieg: Fall of Poland; Dunkirk: 338,000 soldiers saved; Lend-Lease: War goods to allies.

Summary
1. The Germans used a blitzkrieg. In this "lightning war" tactic, air power is used swiftly in combination with land forces.
2. Hitler called off the attacks because he couldn't break British defenses. The British radar system warned of the coming attacks. The British also broke the German army's secret code. Germany finally gave up.
3. The Germans pushed deep into the Soviet Union but were stopped from taking Leningrad. They were forced to retreat.
4. Possible response: The U.S. sold weapons to Britain and France, fired on German submarines, and issued the Atlantic Charter with Britain.

Graphic Organizer
Possible responses:
1. Hitler: removal of threat of attack from the east, division of Poland
   Stalin: division of Poland, takeover of Finland and Baltic countries, safety from German attack
2. *blitzkrieg,* or "lightning war," using fast-moving mechanized weapons and overwhelming force
3. pave a way to France and distract Allies by invading Holland, Belgium, and

Luxembourg, then send massive force through the Ardennes

4. Britain rescued Allied soldiers stranded at Dunkirk and ferried them to safety across the English channel.

5. RAF fighters and British resistance forced Germany to call off the attack.

6. By the beginning of 1942, the British had forced Rommel to retreat. By the middle of the year, however, Rommel pushed the British back and seized Tobruk.

7. In both invasions, Russia's terrible winter and its strategy of destroying everything in the enemy's path created severe hardships for the invaders.

SECTION 2

As You Read

Sample answer: Attack on Pearl Harbor—U.S. enters the war; Attack on Tokyo—Japan shown to be vulnerable; Battle of Midway— Significant Allied victory; Battle of Guadalcanal—Long and bloody struggle.

Summary

1. It declared war on Japan and its allies.
2. China, Burma, Guam, Wake, the Philippine Islands, Indonesia, Malaya, and Singapore
3. Three Allied victories against Japan were the Battle of the Coral Sea, the Battle of Midway, and the Battle of Guadalcanal.

Graphic Organizer

Possible responses:

1. a. Japanese launched surprise attack, sinking or damaging almost the entire U.S. Pacific fleet.
   b. U.S. declared war on Japan.
2. a. Through a planned series of attacks in the Pacific, Japan seized control of rich European colonies.
   b. helped Japan replenish depleted resources
3. a. As revenge for Pearl Harbor, U.S. sent 16 B-25 bombers to bomb Japanese cities.
   b. showed that Japan could be attacked and raised American morale

4. a. Following interception of Japanese attack on Port Moresby, Japanese and American naval fleets fought to a draw.
   b. introduced a new kind of naval warfare using only airplanes; stopped Japan's expansion southward
5. a. American carrier planes defeated Japanese fleet poised to attack Midway Island, a key American airfield.
   b. reversed the tide of war in the Pacific
6. a. U.S. marines, with Australian support, seized Japanese airfield and fought on land and sea for control of island of Guadalcanal.
   b. forced Japan to abandon island of Guadalcanal; began MacArthur's island-hopping counterattack.

SECTION 3

As You Read

Sample answer: Nuremberg Laws; *Kristallnacht,* ghettos, concentration camps.

Summary

1. Hitler's ideas about the superiority of German peoples and his hatred of Jews led to the Holocaust. Early persecution of Jews started with laws taking away their rights and *Kristallnacht*.
2. Jews were taken to extermination camps where they were put to death in huge gas chambers.

Graphic Organizer

Possible responses:

1. "non-Aryan" peoples, primarily Jews; Aryans
2. German laws depriving Jews of rights to citizenship and jobs
   On *Kristallnacht*, the Nazis launched a violent attack on Jewish communities all over Germany.
   systematic murder of entire groups of people, particularly Jews, whom the Nazis saw as inferior
3. France, Britain, the United States, and other countries
   in ghettos—segregated Jewish areas mainly in Germany and Poland
4. to protect the purity of the Aryan race

to carry out mass murders in huge gas chambers
5. early 1942
6. by hiding Jews in their homes or helping them escape to neutral countries approximately 6,000,000

SECTION 4
As You Read
Sample answer: El Alamein: Rommel defeated; Stalingrad: Tide of war turns on the eastern front; D-Day: The recapture of Western Europe began.

Summary
1. The Allies forced the Germans out of Africa. The Red Army forced the Germans to surrender at Stalingrad. The Americans and British forced the Italians to surrender.
2. Japanese Americans who lived on the West Coast were placed in relocation camps.
3. *Possible response:* D-Day, the Battle of the Bulge, the surrounding of Berlin, and the suicide of Hitler.
4. *Possible response:* the Battle of Leyte Gulf, the defeat at Iwo Jima, the defeat at Okinawa, the bombing of Hiroshima, and the bombing of Nagasaki.

Graphic Organizer
Possible responses:
1. forced Rommel and his forces to retreat westward from Egypt 2. landed American troops in North Africa; finally crushed Rommel's Afrika Korps
3. put German forces on the defensive with the Soviets, pushing them westward
4. resulted in Allied conquest of Sicily and forced eventual surrender of Italy
5. rallied people on the home front to do their part to support the war effort
6. opened a second front in Europe; led to the liberation of France, Belgium, Luxembourg, and much of the Netherlands from Nazi occupation
7. German offensive forced Allies to retreat; Allied resistance stopped Germans and resulted in heavy losses for Hitler.
8. wiped out the Japanese navy

9. resulted in heavy losses for Japanese and moved Allies closer to an invasion of Japanese homeland
10. forced surrender of Japan and the end of war

SECTION 5
As You Read
Sample answer: Europe: More displaced persons, famine, communism; Japan: New constitution, radiation from atomic weapons; Both: Death and destruction.

Summary
1. *Possible response:* Widespread suffering, food and fuel shortages, destruction of cities and much countryside, homeless civilians, unemployment
2. The Nuremberg Trials were trials at which Nazi leaders were charged and with crimes against humanity.
3. The government of Japan now had a constitution and a parliament. Everyone over 20, including women, got the right to vote.

Graphic Organizer
Possible responses:
1. destroyed cities, factories, farmland, and utilities, resulting in a ruined economy, shortages, famine, disease, unemployment, and destroyed lives
2. displaced persons, discredited governments, lack of political leadership, threat of Communist takeovers
3. put Nazis on trial for "crimes against humanity"
4. destroyed cities, shattered economy, caused deaths of two million people
5. Government was democratized, land ownership was expanded, standing army was disbanded, and independent labor unions were formed.
6. two-house parliament (Diet) elected by the people, prime minister chosen by majority of Diet as head of government, a vote for all citizens over 20, Japan forbidden to start an offensive war

Restructuring the Postwar World

SECTION 1

As You Read

Sample answer: 1945: Yalta Conference; 1945: United Nations; 1946: Iron Curtain; 1947: Truman Doctrine; 1947: Marshall Plan; 1948: Berlin Airlift; 1949: NATO; 1955: Warsaw Pact; 1960: U-2 incident.

Summary

1. The Soviet Union and the United States had political differences. The Americans wanted to create new markets and encourage democracy. The Soviets wanted to set up Communist governments in Europe to make sure they did not get attacked from the West again.
2. Albania, Bulgaria, Hungary, Czechoslovakia, Romania, Poland, and Yugoslavia
3. The Berlin Airlift occurred when the Soviets cut off all highway and train traffic into Berlin. The United States and Britain flew goods and supplies into the city for 11 months. The Soviets then ended their blockade.
4. Possible Responses: the formation of NATO and the Warsaw Pact; the development of nuclear weapons; *Sputnik,* and the U-2 incident.

Graphic Organizer

Possible responses:

1. When pressed by Truman to allow free elections in Eastern Europe, Stalin refused and later declared that war between the two powers was certain.
2. Designed to halt the spread of communism, the policy resulted in the United States assisting weak countries to resist Soviet advances.
3. U.S. support for countries that rejected communism intensified diplomatic hostility between the two superpowers.
4. By helping Western Europe rebuild, the United States made possible future

resistance to Communist expansion in Europe.

5. led to Berlin airlift and Soviet admission of defeat
6. led to formation of Warsaw Pact and division of Europe into two rival military camps
7. brought the two superpowers closer to the edge of war
8. led to rivalry between the two superpowers in science and education

SECTION 2

As You Read

Sample answer: 1. Civil war—Two Chinas; 2. Superpowers reacted—Soviets supported Communists, U.S. supported Taiwan; 3. Communists controlled mainland—China expanded; 4. Mandate of Heaven—Reshaped economy; 5. Great Leap Forward—Failure of economy; 6. Cultural Revolution—destruction of intellectual, artistic base.

Summary

1. The Communists, led by Mao Zedong, fought against the Nationalists, led by Jiang Jieshi.
2. The United States sided with the Nationalists, and the Soviets helped the Communists.
3. Possible responses: redistribution of land, creation of collective farms, control of industry, and the Cultural Revolution.

Graphic Organizer

Possible responses:

1. leader of Communist forces and later chairman of the Communist party and head of People's Republic of China; leader of Nationalist forces and later head of Republic of China
2. end of WWII; 1949
3. large army, U.S. aid; army skilled in guerrilla warfare, popular support
4. on island of Taiwan; on mainland China
5. United States helped Nationalists set up government and enlarged American sphere of influence in Asia; Soviets provided Communist China financial, military and technical aid and signed a defensive

alliance. Mao transformed China's economy by giving land to peasants, forming collective farms, and nationalizing businesses.

6. because of poor planning, inefficient industries, lack of work incentive, crop failures and famine; to revive the Marxist revolution he had begun

SECTION 3
As You Read
Sample answer: Korean War: Neither side gained an advantage; Vietnam War: Soviet-supported North Vietnamese won; Both: U.S. and Soviet involvement stemmed from Cold War, land was destroyed, millions of people died.

Summary
1. It didn't; the division between North and South Korea remained the same.
2. North Vietnam overran the South and made Vietnam one country again, this time under a Communist government.

Graphic Organizer
Possible responses:
1. South Korea asked the UN to intervene when North Koreans crossed the 38th parallel and attacked.
2. Communist North Korea became a military power but declined economically; South Korea became industrialized and prospered economically with the help of U.S. aid.
3. After the Japanese lost World War II, nationalists wanted independence, but France wanted to regain its colony.
4. The French were defeated at Dien Bien Phu and surrendered to Ho Chi Minh. An international peace conference divided Vietnam.
5. Fearing the overthrow of the anti-Communist government it helped set up in South Vietnam, the United States escalated its military involvement.
6. Unable to win a decisive victory, the United States withdrew in response to intense pressure at home.

SECTION 4
As You Read
Sample answer: Cuba: Communist revolution overthrows dictator, invasion by U.S.-backed forces repulsed; Nicaragua: Communist revolution overthrows dictator, elections held; Iran: Islamic revolution overthrows dictator, fundamentalist Islamic republic established.

Summary
1. Third World nations faced political unrest, poverty, and poor education and technology.
2. Communists gained power in Cuba and in Nicaragua.
3. Khomeini made Islamic law the law of the land; followed a foreign policy strongly against the United States; and led his country to a long war with Iraq.

Graphic Organizer
Possible responses:
1. At first, the economy, health care, and literacy improved; however, a harsh dictatorship violated basic rights.
2. U.S. relations with Cuba had deteriorated as a result of Castro's economic policies.
3. U.S. blockade of Cuba and troops on alert in Florida led Khrushchev to remove missiles in return for a U.S. promise not to invade Cuba.
4. a weakened economy and political unrest
5. The United States had supported the shah and the westernization of Iran.
6. secretly sold arms to Iran
7. Both were costly wars that lasted longer than expected; both resulted in superpowers being overpowered by rebel forces.

SECTION 5
As You Read
Sample answer: I. A. Destalinization, B. Revolt in Hungary, C. Revolt in Czechoslovakia, D. Soviet-Chinese split; II. A. U-2 incident, B. Cuban missile crisis, C. Escalation of Vietnam War, D. End of Vietnam War, E. Nixon's China trip, F. SALT

I treaty; III. The Collapse of Détente, A. Non-ratification of SALT II, B. SDI.

Summary

1. The Soviets put down revolts in Hungary and Czechoslovakia.
2. *Possible responses:* the Soviet invasion of Afghanistan, the election of Reagan, Reagan's anti-missile program, and U.S. support for rebels fighting Communists in Nicaragua.

Graphic Organizer

Possible responses:

1. Nagy formed a new government and ordered Soviet troops to leave.
2. Dubcek tried to reform communism and give it a "human face."
3. began spreading its own version of communism in parts of Asia and Africa
4. brinkmanship
5. brinkmanship
6. détente and realpolitik
7. retreated from détente and heightened tensions between superpowers
8. reduce tensions and prevent nuclear war
9. limit number of ICBMs and submarine-launched missiles in each country
10. to protect the United States against enemy missiles

The Colonies Become New Nations

SECTION 1

As You Read

Sample answer: Jawaharlal Nehru, Indira Gandhi, Rajiv Gandhi, Manmohan Singh

Summary

1. *Possible responses:* nationalists realized colonial rulers could be defeated; people questioned the right of nations to control colonies.
2. People had only one month to decide which country to live in. Millions of people began to move to different regions. Violence broke out.
3. India and Pakistan continue to fight over Kashmir because the Muslims of the

region do not like being ruled by India, which is controlled by Hindus.
4. Possible responses: Pakistan's division into east and west parts led to a civil war, in which the eastern part won its independence and took the name Bangladesh. There have violent power struggles in Pakistan since then.

Graphic Organizer

Possible responses:

1. that the Congress Party would primarily protect Hindu interests
2. movement of millions of people to new homes; division of courts, military, civil service; violence among religious groups
3. placed a third of Kashmir under Pakistani control and the rest under Indian control
4. pushed for industrialization and social reforms; tried to elevate status of lower castes and improve women's rights
5. civil war in Pakistan and withdrawal of West Pakistan army from East Pakistan
6. acts of violence from Sikh extremists agitating for independence
7. a civil war between Tamil militants and the Sri Lankan government

SECTION 2

As You Read

Sample answer: Philippines: Election corruption, power abuse, rebel groups; Burma: Repressive military; Malaysia: Ethnic differences, Communist uprising; Indonesia: Many islands, ethnic groups, languages, and religions; East Timor: Conflict over independence.

Summary

1. Marcos was the leader of the Philippines from 1966 to 1986 who, though elected, ruled as a dictator and was eventually forced to step down.
2. Since 1962, generals have ruled the country. Burma changed its name to Myanmar in 1989. Violence continues to trouble the country.
3. Indonesia is so spread out that it is hard to unify the country. It has 13,600 islands

and includes people from 300 different groups speaking 250 languages.

Graphic Organizer

Possible responses:

1. an agreement to establish free trade between the United States and the Philippines for eight years followed by gradually increasing tariffs
    a. feared American exploitation of Philippine resources and environment
    b. could not get money for war damages until they signed the act
2. to protect its economic and security interests in Asia
3. to prevent the abuse of power that occurred during the 20-year rule of Ferdinand Marcos
4. a. set up repressive military government in 1962
    b. won majority of seats in legislature in 1990 election that was not recognized by military government
5. a. independent city b. -and c. members of Federation of Malaysia
6. growing unrest over his regressive policies and a crippling economic crisis

SECTION 3

As You Read

Sample answer: Ghana: Nkrumah damaged economy through costly projects; Kenya: Kenyatta fought against British; Zaire: Mobutu overthrown; Algeria: French colonists fought independence, long civil war; Angola: Portuguese fought to keep county but gave up, long civil war.

Summary

1. The Negritude movement was a movement among Africans after World War II. Its purpose was to celebrate African culture, heritage, and values.
2. In Ghana, Nkrumah faced opposition to his plans for economic growth and the army that seized power. In Kenya, Kenyatta faced the difficulty of trying to unite many different peoples in one country. Later, Kenya faced the problems of violence and a weak economy.

3. Mobutu Sese Seko's rule was harsh and corrupt. He helped impoverish his country.

Graphic Organizer

Possible responses:

1. organized strikes and boycotts; developed industry and expensive health, welfare, and education programs; economic and political instability
2. frightened white farmers, forcing them to leave farmland in northern highlands; tried to unite ethnic and language groups, developed business; civil disorder
3. granted suddenly by Belgium; brutal and corrupt rule; depleted resources, extreme poverty, social unrest
4. France transferred power after 1962 referendum; began land reforms, developed plans for education; unemployment, Islamic revival and ensuing civil war
5. assumed when Portuguese troops withdrew; Communist seizure of power and fighting among rebel groups supported by outside sources; continuing tension among groups and foreign countries supporting them

SECTION 4

As You Read

Sample answer: Suez Crisis; Six-Day War; Yom Kippur war; PLO formed; Camp David Accords; Sadat killed; first intifada; second intifada.

Summary

1. Israel was created out of the Palestine Mandate in land that had been the ancient homeland of the Jewish people. Muslims had occupied the land since the 7th century. These two groups fought over who should control the land.
2. *Possible response:* Both were wars started by the Arab nations to regain territory lost to other peoples—Europeans and Israelis. The Arab nations lost both wars.
3. The Camp David Accords were the first signed peace agreement between Israel and an Arab country.

4. Possible response: Although both sides have made progress toward peace, violence still occurs.

Graphic Organizer
Possible responses:
1. Causes: increased immigration of Jews to Palestine, request for a Jewish homeland Effects: no resolution of issue; British referral of Palestine issue to UN
2. Causes: UN recommendation calling for a partition of the Palestine Mandate; international sympathy for Jews because of Holocaust and support for their desire for a Jewish state Effects: outbreak of full-scale Arab-Israeli war
3. Causes: Egypt's seizure of Suez Canal Effects: defeat of Egyptians; as a result of world pressure, withdrawal of Israel and its European allies from Egypt
4. Causes: increased tensions between Israel and Arab states; movement of Soviet-backed Arab forces off Gulf of Aqaba Effects: heavy Arab losses; Israeli annexation of old city of Jerusalem, West Bank, Sinai Peninsula, and Golan Heights
5. Causes: joint Arab attack on holiest Jewish holiday Effects: Israeli counterattack followed by an uneasy truce
6. Causes: Sadat's offer of peace to Israel; Carter's invitation to Sadat and Begin to discuss divisive issues at Camp David Effects: Egyptian recognition of Israel as a legitimate nation, transfer of Sinai Peninsula to Egypt, end of 30 years of hostilities, assassination of Sadat
7. Causes: ongoing conflict over Israeli-occupied territories, which led to a series of peace talks Effects: self-rule for Palestinians in Gaza Strip and West Bank; assassination of Rabin

SECTION 5
As You Read
Sample answer: I. A. Economic struggles, B. Ethnic and religious strife. II. A. Fight for independence, B. Taliban brings Islamic fundamentalism, C. Support for terrorism.

Summary
1. They relied greatly on the Soviets for economic help, and thus struggled to stand on their own when the Soviet Union collapsed.
2. Taliban leaders forbade women to go to school or hold jobs; they prohbited watching television or movies or listening to modern music.

Graphic Organizer
Possible responses:
1. These nations relied heavily on the Soviet Union for economic help, so they have had trouble being on their own. Also, economic practices forced on some regions by the Soviet Union led to additional problems.
2. There are many different peoples living in Central Asia, some of which have a long history of hostility toward one another. Soviet rule kept these enmities in check, but they have erupted anew since the Soviet Union's demise.
3. Britain wanted to gain control over Afghanistan to protect the northern border of colonial India. Russia wanted access to the Indian Ocean through Afghanistan.
4. to battle against the mujahideen—the "holy warriors" who were fighting against the Communist regime that had seized control of Afghanistan.
5. Taliban rule brought order, limited corruption, and promoted business. However, the Taliban, through its extreme interpretation of Islam, severely restricted women's rights, banned free expression, and instituted gruesome, medieval punishments for legal infractions. It also allowed terror groups to live and train in Afghanistan.

6. It invaded the country and gave assistance to anti-Taliban groups, such as the Northern Alliance.

Struggles for Democracy

SECTION 1
As You Read
Sample answer: Brazil: Direct elections; Mexico: Democratic constitution; Argentina: Civilian government.

Summary
1. *Possible responses:* free and fair elections; more than one political party; an educated population; a common culture; acceptance of the idea of equal rights; and rule by law.
2. Land reform gave land to peasants but brought resistance from landowners who backed a group that took power and created military rule.
3. The PRI has controlled Mexico through the local, state, and national governments. The PRI has acted harshly to stop dissent. Recently, however, the PRI opened the government to other parties. In 2000, the PRI lost power to Vicente Fox.
4. The army controlled the Argentine government for many years after Perón was overthrown. The army ruled harshly and killed many people in the opposition.

Graphic Organizer
Possible responses:
1. free and open elections, majority rule, citizen participation; constitutional government
2. stable economy, belief in individual rights, rule by law
3. developed industry, encouraged foreign investments, redistributed land
4. free elections of civilian government
5. massacre of protesters in Aztec ruins, economic decline following drop in oil prices
6. election of Vicente Fox ended 71 years of PRI rule

7. ruined economy, increased acts of terrorism, brutal suppression of basic rights and freedoms
8. free elections

SECTION 2
As You Read
Sample answer: Nigeria: Civil war when Biafra seceded; South Africa: Passage of apartheid; Both: Former British colonies.

Summary
1. *Possible responses:* Europeans drew up borders in Africa that paid no attention to ethnic groupings, leading to ethnic conflict. The Europeans did not develop the African economies. The colonies lacked a middle class and skilled workers.
2. The Nigerian civil war was followed by a period of martial law. In 1979, military rule gave way to an elected government. But military leaders overthrew this government in 1983.
3. The ANC was formed to fight for the rights of black South Africans.
4 De Klerk ended apartheid because of a rising tide of resistance and violence as well as international opposition and economic pressure.

Graphic Organizer
Possible responses:
1. lack of national identity; continuing ethnic and cultural rivalries, some of them leading to civil wars
2. unbalanced economies, small middle class, few products for local consumption
3. creation of new nation of Biafra, destruction of Igbo region, death of millions, and later, establishment of a more stable federal government
4. end of democracy, Hausa-Fulani discrimination against other ethnic groups
5. promotion of Afrikaner nationalism and establishment of apartheid policy
6. government repression of protesters; protests that led to South African government declaring a state of emergency

7. legalization of the ANC, release of Nelson Mandela from prison, and a new era in South Africa

8. victory for ANC and election of Mandela as president

SECTION 3
As You Read
Sample answer: 1985–1987: Gorbachev introduces glasnost; 1991: coup attempt; 1992: Yeltsin's "shock therapy" begins; 1994: Russian forces destroy Chechen capital, Grozny; 2000: Putin elected president.

Summary
1. Glasnost meant opening up Soviet society in a number of ways. Churches were allowed to open, dissidents were released from prison, banned authors were allowed to publish, reporters were allowed to investigate and criticize officials.

2. Perestroika involved restructuring the Soviet economy. In general, it tried to improve the Soviet economy by lifting the tight controls on managers and workers.

3. Possible answers: the uprising in Lithuania; calls from many ethnic groups for separate nationhood; shifting support from Gorbachev to Yeltsin; the 1991 coup; the banning of the Communist Party from political activity; and declarations of independence by various republics.

4. Yeltsin tried shock therapy, an abrupt move toward capitalism.

5. High rates of unemployment, domestic violence, and homeless children, as well as declining population, life expectancy, and standard of living.

Graphic Organizer
Possible responses:
1. initiated glasnost policy, encouraging a free flow of ideas and information
2. introduced perestroika, giving managers more authority over their farms and factories and allowing for creation of small private businesses
3. signed the INF treaty with President Reagan

4. Hard-liners demanded Gorbachev's resignation; protesters appealed to Yeltsin to oppose the coup; Yeltsin mobilized support against the coup; troops refused to obey hard-liners; the coup failed and Gorbachev returned to Moscow.

5. After the coup, Estonia and Latvia declared their independence; other republics soon followed; Yeltsin met with leaders of republics to chart new course; they formed the Commonwealth of Independent States.

6. Yeltsin adopted "shock therapy" to deal with the ailing Russian economy; this involved an abrupt shift to free-market economics; he lowered trade barriers, removed price controls, and ended subsidies to state industries.

7. Yeltsin denied Chechnya's right to secede; he ordered Russian troops into Chechnya; despite a cease fire, the fighting flared up again and Yeltsin resigned as the fighting raged; Vladimir Putin attempted to deal forcefully with the rebellion in Chechnya; the fighting dragged on.

SECTION 4
As You Read
Sample answer: Yugoslavia: Ethnic tensions, loss of Tito's authority, Serbian aggression; Czechoslovakia: Economic problems.

Summary
1. The Polish people became frustrated over how difficult the transition to democracy and capitalism was.

2. The Communists lost power in East Germany, and the following year German reunification took place.

3. Communist rule ended in Czechoslovakia after large protests; eventually the country broke into two separate nations: the Czech Republic and Slovakia.

4. Communism ended in Romania after bloody fighting. A reform government introduced elements of capitalism into the economy in order to improve it.

5. After the Slovenians and Croatians declared independence from Yugoslavia,

the Serbs fought against them to keep them in the nation. The Slovenians and Croatians won. The Serbs also fought against the Muslims of Bosnia-Herzegovina.

Graphic Organizer
Possible responses:
1. Many Poles were unhappy with the slow pace of economic progress.
2. Reformers encouraged private enterprise, allowed a stock market to operate, allowed a multiparty system with free election.
3. When the East German government closed its borders, protesters demanded the right to travel freely and the right to vote in free elections.
4. An economic reform program caused a sharp rise in unemployment that especially hurt Slovakia. Unable to agree on economic policy, the country's two parts drifted apart (into the Czech Republic and Slovakia).
5. He ordered the army to fire on demonstrators who were demanding reform; hundreds of people were killed and wounded; the massacre ignited a popular uprising against Ceausescu.

SECTION 5
As You Read
Sample answer: 1971: Zhou opens China to West; 1980s: Four Modernizations.

Summary
1. Mao's economic programs failed to create economic growth.
2. Deng's changes helped people have more income and allowed them to purchase more goods.
3. Thousands of protesters were killed or wounded by army troops and tanks.
4. People worry that China will not respect Hong Kong's freedom.
5. Economic reform came first. China has managed to reduce poverty and introduce elements of a market economy without a great deal of political reform. Political reform is likely to follow improved economic and social conditions.

Graphic Organizer
Possible responses:
1. Goals: to rid China of anti-revolutionary forces who want to modernize the economy
   Outcomes: economic, political, and social chaos; increased opposition to radical communism and party leadership
2. Goals: to end China's isolation and form ties with the West
   Outcomes: ushered in a new era in Chinese-American relations; led to cultural exchanges, limited trade, and formal diplomatic relations
3. Goals: to improve China's economy
   Outcomes: increase in food and industrial production, higher standard of living, widening gap between rich and poor, exposure to Western political ideas
4. Goals: to end dictatorship and create a democracy in China
   Outcomes: brutal repression of pro-democracy movement, international awareness of human rights violations in China
5. Goals: to end colonial rule
   Outcomes: fear that Hong Kong citizens will lose freedom; reinforcement of Chinese identity for many citizens

Global Interdependence
SECTION 1
As You Read
Sample answer: Communications: Worldwide television, home offices/telecommuting; Health and Medicine: Improved diagnoses and surgery; Green Revolution: Increased crop yields, decreased use of pesticides.

Summary
1. Cooperation included the docking of U.S. and Soviet spacecraft in 1975, American-Soviet space missions including scientists from other countries, and the building of the International Space Station.
2. Computer chips are found in everyday objects such as microwave ovens, telephones, and cars. Millions of people

use computers at home. Many of the people use computers that are connected to the Internet.

3. Genetic engineering enables scientists to use genes in new ways. This has led to advances in agriculture and medicine.

Graphic Organizer

Possible responses:

1. launching of manned and unmanned space shuttles and commercial satellites to explore space; exploration of moon; docking of two spacecrafts in space; the International Space Station

2. construction and launching of the Hubble Space Telescope and space probes such as *Pathfinder* to Mars

3. miniaturization of the circuitry in computers that made possible personal computers; development of satellite communication, fax machines, the Internet, and e-mail

4. laser surgery; ultrasound, CAT scans, and MRI imaging techniques

5. isolation of individual genes; genetic engineering; cloning

6. increased crop yields through use of fertilizers and pesticides; reproduction and improvement of selected plants through genetic engineering

SECTION 2
As You Read

Sample answer: Advances in communication and transportation; Development of multinational corporations; Expanded free trade; Regional trading agreements.

Summary

1. Jobs in service and information industries are increasing.

2. Steps toward free trade include the establishment of the European Union, NAFTA, and a free trade zone in Latin America.

3. Economic growth has resulted in pollution, acid rain, and weakening of Earth's ozone layer.

Graphic Organizer

Possible responses:

1. Causes: Emerging nations have workers with skills appropriate for manufacturing jobs and who are willing to work for low wages; developed nations need better educated workers for their growing information industries.

2. Effects: A global economy was created.

3. Causes: The European experiment in free trade was successful and made Europe a major force in the world economy.

4. Effects: Disruption in the distribution of oil causes global political problems; pollution, acid rain, and global warming threaten the environment.

5. Effects: The ozone layer in the Earth's upper atmosphere is destroyed, ultraviolet radiation increases, and more incidents of skin cancer occur.

6. Causes: Their habitats are being destroyed by land development.

SECTION 3
As You Read

Sample answer: Formation of the UN: Reduced threat of conflict, promoted peace; Arms-control agreements: Reduced number of weapons of mass destruction.

Summary

1. Two specific approaches are the reduction of weapons of mass destruction and the use of international peacekeeping forces to reduce, prevent, or settle conflicts.

2. *Possible response:* Two important events in the struggle for human rights are the creation of the Universal Declaration of Human Rights and the women's rights movement.

3. Sub-Saharan Africa

4. When people move to other countries, they can sometimes cause problems for the country that may not want to accept them or may have difficulties integrating them into society. Immigrants sometimes suffer hunger or disease or bad conditions in refugee camps.

Graphic Organizer
Possible responses:
1. increased each member nation's security by making an attack on one an attack on all
2. provided a place to mediate and resolve conflicts in any stage of development; provided peace-keeping soldiers to help prevent outbreak of new fighting or to enforce a cease-fire
3. helped to reduce nuclear arsenals and prevent the spread of nuclear weapons to other countries
4. often result in terrible violence and human rights abuses
5. Many people consider a decent standard of health a basic human right. Therefore, poor health is viewed as a threat to global security.
6. set human rights standards for all nations to follow and listed specific rights all humans should have
7. fought discrimination in employment and tried to improve the lives of women through changes in law and government policy
8. gave people an opportunity to escape human rights violations in their countries by migrating to other countries

SECTION 4
As You Read
Sample answer: World Incidents: Munich Olympics, 1972; Tokyo subway attacks, 1995; Bombings of U.S. embassies, 1998.

Summary
1. Bombs, bullets, biological and chemical weapons, computer viruses
2. Civil unrest and regional wars
3. Before September 11, many Americans thought that terrorism was something that happened in other countries. After September 11, many Americans became afraid that terrorist attacks could happen to them.
4. The Federal Aviation Administration (FAA) ordered airlines to put in bars on cockpit doors. These bars would help stop hijackers from getting control of planes. National Guard troops began to guard airports. Trained security officers called sky marshals were put on planes. The Aviation and Transportation Security Act was passed. It put the federal government in charge of airport security.

Graphic Organizer
Possible responses:
1. Osama bin Laden is the leader of a terrorist group called al-Qaeda; trained security officers who fly on planes and protect them from hijackers
2. 1998; September 11, 2001
3. Cyberterrorism consists of politically motivated attacks on information systems. A department of the U.S. government that coordinates national efforts against terrorism
4. the Summer Olympic Games in the Tokyo subway
5. The FAA ordered airlines to install bars on cockpit doors to prevent hijackers from gaining control of the plane. Sky marshals—trained security officers—were assigned to fly on planes, and National Guard troops began patrolling airports. Terrorists flew an airliner into the Pentagon.
6. to oppose British control of Northern Ireland; Critics believe that the USA Patriot Act allows the government to infringe on people's civil rights

SECTION 5
As You Read
Sample answer: Television, movies food, sports, music, art, clothing fashions.

Summary
1. Possible responses: music, sports, clothing styles, food, hobbies, television shows, and interest in popular athletes.
2. The English language has spread, as well as Western clothes and foods. Western materialism has also spread.
3. Cultural blending may begin to erase distinct characteristics of culture and create movements to keep traditions alive.

Graphic Organizer
Possible responses:
1. accelerated the spread of culture to more people over greater distances
2. Television, radio, and movies are the most popular forms of entertainment and information worldwide. Through TV daily newscasts and programming, people in different parts of the world share global events, political drama, and everyday life.
3. Today, the West dominates worldwide mass media and English has become the primary international language; earlier, the West influenced other cultures by colonizing the Americas, Asia, and Africa.
4. Western culture is more materialistic than many non-western cultures.
5. They fear that it will result in the loss of their unique identity as a people or nation.
6. Some countries have adopted policies that reserve television time for national programming. In other countries, television programmers take Western shows and rework them according to their own culture and traditions. In still other countries, people have taken an active role in preserving their traditional ways of life.